ONCE AN ARAFAT MAN

ONCE

THE TRUE STORY OF

AN

HOW A **PLO** SNIPER

ARAFAT

FOUND A NEW LIFE

MAN

TASS SAADA
WITH DEAN MERRILL

TYNDALE HOUSE PUBLISHERS, INC.
CAROL STREAM, ILLINOIS

Visit Tyndale online at www.tyndale.com.

Contact Tass at www.onceanarafatman.com, or visit his organizations' websites at seedsofhopeinc.org and www.hopeforishmael.org.

TYNDALE and Tyndale's quill logo are registered trademarks of Tyndale House Publishers, Inc.

Once an Arafat Man: The True Story of How a PLO Sniper Found a New Life

Adapted from the book *Ich kämpfte für Arafat*, published by Brunnen Verlag Basel under ISBN 978-3-7655-1408-1.

Designed by Erik M. Peterson

Edited by Cara Peterson

Published in association with the literary agency of Riggins International Rights Services, Inc., 1960-J Madison Street, Suite 343, Clarksville, TN 37043.

Scripture taken from the Holy Bible, *New International Version,*® *NIV.*® Copyright © 1973, 1978, 1984 by Biblica, Inc.™ Used by permission of Zondervan. All rights reserved worldwide. www.zondervan.com.

Library of Congress Cataloging-in-Publication Data

Saada, Tass.
    Once an Arafat man : the true story of how a PLO sniper found a new life / Tass Saada ; with Dean Merrill.
        p. cm.
    Includes bibliographical references.
    ISBN 978-1-4143-2361-9 (hc)
    ISBN 978-1-4143-3444-8 (sc)
    1. Saada, Tass.   2. Christian converts from Islam—Biography   I. Merrill, Dean.   II. Title.
    BV2626.4.S23A3 2008
    248.2'46092—dc22
    [B]   2008027390

Printed in the United States of America

15   14   13   12   11
8   7   6   5   4

DEDICATION

To my parents, six brothers, and four
sisters in the Middle East, who will
always be my beloved family.

To my wife, Karen, who showed me
what true love means.

To my son, Ben, his wife, Addie, and my
daughter, Farah—I am so proud of you.

CONTENTS

FOREWORD

LET ME BE BRUTALLY HONEST.

Tass Saada was a killer. That's why the first section of this book was incredibly difficult for me to read. This is not *Anne of Green Gables*. This is not *The Sound of Music*. If you're looking for a light, romantic story about growing up in the gorgeous splendor of Prince Edward Island, Canada, or about climbing every mountain in Austria—singing as you go—then move on, dear reader. This book is not for you.

Tass and his closest friends murdered Jews in Israel. They murdered civilians and soldiers alike. They attacked Christians in Jordan. Sometimes they tossed hand grenades at their homes. Sometimes they strafed God-fearing homes with machine-gun fire. They once tried to assassinate the crown prince of an Arab country. They nearly succeeded. And they did all this willingly. They did so eagerly. Tass certainly did. His nickname was once *Jazzar*—"butcher." It was a moniker he relished.

Born in Gaza and raised in Saudi Arabia and the Persian Gulf in a world of radical Islam and violent Palestinian nationalism, by his teenage years Tass was a cauldron of seething, roiling hatred. His family was close to the Saudi royal family. He once met Osama bin Laden. He became personal friends with Yasser Arafat, a man he long regarded as a hero, and happily killed in his name. In part one of the book you hold in your hands, Tass takes you inside the world he once loved. It is not pretty. Indeed, for me it was painful in a way that is almost impossible to convey adequately in the vocabulary of the English language.

If Tass's story ended there, there would be no way I could endorse it, much less write its foreword. But it doesn't end there. In his amazing grace, God gave Tass Saada a second act. And a third.

What follows, then, is the unforgettable story of a jihadist who found Jesus, of a violent revolutionary who was radically transformed one day by the power of the Holy Spirit and became a man of peace and compassion. At its core, this is a story of the greatness of our great God. It is the story of a man who fell in love with a Savior who loves Arabs as well as Jews. The God of the Bible is crystal clear to all who will listen: he loves us all with an unfathomable love, with an everlasting love, with an unquenchable love. His love is so amazing, so divine that he actually offers all of us—Jew and Gentile alike—the free gift of salvation through the death and resurrection of his Son, Jesus Christ our Lord. He wants to adopt each one of us into his own family. He wants to bless us. He wants to take care of us. He wants to heal us and change us and make us like him. And then he wants to empower us to be a blessing to others.

Tass said yes to that love, and he was changed forever. I won't spoil it for you by giving all the good stuff away. Suffice it to say: Read this book quickly! Get through the first section as fast as you can and get to the turning point. See how God not only changed Tass's life but his family's as well. Be at his side as he is called into the ministry, as he shares the gospel with Yasser Arafat, and even as he shares the message of Christ's love and forgiveness with his parents and brothers, who all want to kill him. As the story progresses, see Tass and his lovely wife, Karen, as they reach out to the poor and needy in Gaza and the West Bank in the name of Jesus. And watch how Tass's heart changes towards the Jews. This part I can personally vouch for.

Tass and I met on a Saturday night in January 2008. I had been invited to preach at a Messianic Jewish congregation in Jerusalem that night. My sermon title was "What God Is Doing among the Muslims." This is not a typical message for a Jewish audience. But after much prayer, I felt the Lord wanted me to share with my Israeli friends what he had told me to share with my Jordanian friends when I had preached in Amman not long before: We need to get serious about obeying Jesus' command to love our neighbors and our enemies. We can only do this when we have the power of the Holy Spirit flowing through our lives. But when we do—when we truly obey the words and model of Jesus—heads will turn. People will be shocked when they see us love those who hate us. Then they will ask questions. Their hearts will be softened. They will be curious to know more about the God we serve. And then, hopefully, they will want to know this God personally for themselves.

We are already seeing it happen, all over the Middle East. More Muslims are coming to faith in Jesus Christ over the last ten to fifteen years—and particularly since 9/11—than at any other time in human history. The question for Israeli believers and for all of us who claim to be followers of Jesus is this: What role does the Lord have for us in strengthening our brothers and sisters who come to Christ from a Muslim background, and how can we actively love our neighbors and our enemies when humanly speaking this is impossible?

That was the message I came to share in Jerusalem, and who was the first couple I was introduced to that night as I came in the front door of the congregation? Tass and Karen Saada. When I was told who they were, I could hardly believe it. When they gave me an executive summary of their story, I was deeply moved. Here we were, a former aide to PLO Chairman Yasser Arafat and a former aide to Prime Minister Benjamin Netanyahu, hugging each other—not trying to kill each other—in the heart of Jerusalem. All because of the work Jesus had done to give us hearts of love rather than hatred.

I had a sense that this was the beginning of a story, not the end. So the next day we decided to travel together with several other colleagues to the Israeli city of Ashkelon. There we visited a hospital that treats Jews and Arabs wounded in the ongoing border skirmishes that have plagued that region for so long. As we met with the hospital administrators, we both presented checks from our respective ministries to help finance the purchase of desperately needed medical equipment. When the doctors and staff asked why we had come to bless them, we both told them our stories. Tass explained that he had been born just a few miles south of where we were gathered, and raised with a desire to kill everyone in the room where we were sitting.

"You really worked for the PLO?" asked one doctor.

Tass nodded.

"Then what happened? What changed you?" another asked.

Tass gave all the credit to Jesus Christ. He briefly explained how God had changed his heart and given him a love for the Jewish people. And then he stunned us all. He asked the hospital staff to forgive him for what he and the Palestinian people had done over the years to harm them. It was a powerful moment. Everyone was in tears. These Israelis had never seen anything like it, and honestly, neither had I.

As you read this book, please pray for Tass and Karen and their family and team, and enlist others to pray for them too. Pray for their safety. Pray for continued courage. Pray for wisdom and discernment. Pray Colossians 4:2-4 for them:

> Devote yourselves to prayer, being watchful and thankful.
> And pray for us, too, that God may open a door for our
> message, so that we may proclaim the mystery of Christ,
> for which I am in chains. Pray that I may proclaim it clearly,
> as I should.

Pray for open doors for the Saadas to share the good news of Christ's radical love with many more in Gaza, the West Bank, and throughout the Muslim world. Pray, too, that the Lord would bless them with the physical, spiritual, and emotional strength and energy they need to do his work, and that he would bless them with the financial resources they need to advance the gospel and care for the poor.

Finally, please pray about what God is calling you to do. Are you loving your neighbors? Are you making disciples of *all* nations, as Jesus commands us in Matthew 28:18-20? Are you praying for the Palestinian people, and for Muslims everywhere, to find new life and new hope in Jesus? Are you investing in the work of ministries like Hope for Ishmael?

You and I are living at a remarkable moment in human history. Before Jesus returns, God the Father is drawing men, women, and children to himself as never before. He is doing something absolutely astounding and unprecedented among the Muslim people. Why not join him? Why not be part of the spiritual revolution that is saving souls and making true peace in Jesus' name? Personally, I cannot think of a greater adventure of which to be a part. Perhaps the fact that you are about to read this book suggests you think so, too.

–JOEL C. ROSENBERG
Washington, DC
July 2008

Joel C. Rosenberg is the founder of The Joshua Fund, a humanitarian relief organization whose mission is "to bless Israel and her neighbors in the name of Jesus, according to Genesis 12:1-3." He is also the *New York Times* best-selling author of six books, including *The Last Jihad* and *Epicenter: Why the Current Rumblings in the Middle East Will Change Your Future.*

NOTE TO THE READER

HAVE YOU EVER ACTUALLY MET A PALESTINIAN? I admit I had not, until I began working on this project. Like many other Americans, I had simply drawn a few conclusions (mostly negative) from what I saw or read in the news. These were the people, I told myself, who didn't like Israel and kept fussing about it year after year.

Then I met Tass Saada. I was brought face to face with his gentle spirit and that of his gracious wife, Karen. I heard the story of how he had been born in a refugee tent, gotten pushed around from place to place as he grew up, and was finally radicalized into taking up arms against what he viewed as the unfairness of it all. I put myself in his shoes. I would no doubt have felt the same as he did, and taken action.

But that was only the beginning. I became intrigued with his coming to the United States at age twenty-three, getting married, and succeeding in the business world. His midlife discovery of what to do about the fires of hatred that burned inside him fascinated me. The longer he talked, the more I saw a grand purpose for this man's life.

The Tass Saada I know today is not a hater. He's more of a big teddy bear who understands what will bring calm to the Middle East. He knows that political bantering can go only so far. He sees beyond the shouts and bomb blasts to the true wellsprings of harmony that will relieve bitterness and result in lasting peace.

In this he offers a parable for every human being's private turmoil. Many of us, like the adversaries in the Holy Land, have people in our lives we simply wish would go away. But of course, that isn't going to happen. So what do we do next? Read on. . . .

—DEAN MERRILL,
coauthor

ACKNOWLEDGMENTS

A BOOK IS NEVER CONCOCTED OUT OF THIN AIR. It is the product of a life. And a life such as mine has been greatly shaped by people who came alongside me.

None of this would have been worth writing without the incredible influence of **Charlie Sharpe** during more than thirty years now. He came into my life when I was a new immigrant, and he stayed with me until he led me to life's most important crossroad. Since then he has continued to be my mentor, my spiritual counsel, my great friend. I will always appreciate him and his wife, **Laurie,** for their impact on my life and work.

My story first appeared in book form in the German language under the title *Ich kämpfte für Arafat* (2007), published by Brunnen Verlag, a Swiss publisher. Many thanks to **Christian Meyer** and **Vera Hahn** as well as coauthor **Daniel Gerber** for making this happen.

Then **Cindy Riggins** made the vital connection with Tyndale House to consider an English rendition, which you now hold in your hands. There, **Jon Farrar** and his colleagues became excited about the potential. I am grateful for them all.

The conversion to English turned into a complete rewrite as well as an update and expansion. For this, I want to thank **Dean Merrill,** who brought his journalistic skill to bear. In the process, he has become a dear friend and brother.

Neither German nor English is my mother tongue, of course. That is all the more reason why I am thankful for those who have helped me communicate in these languages.

—TASS SAADA

PART 1

HOW
I
LEARNED
TO
HATE

CHAPTER 1

THE SECOND BATTLE OF JERICHO

THE MORNING SUN FELT WARM ON MY BACK as I crouched behind a large pile of shrubbery I had scraped together, overlooking the Jordan River valley. Jericho, perhaps the world's oldest city, lay across the river in the distance. Here on the east side, my comrades and I had spent the night in a chilly cave along this range of hills. Now we were up early and excited about the surprise we would deliver to the advancing IDF (Israel Defense Forces) troops. My sleek, high-powered Simonov rifle with its telescopic sight lay beside me on the ground as I gazed down upon the quiet town of al-Karameh.

The dirt roads that meandered among the humble, mud-brick homes with flat roofs were empty on this morning of March 21, 1968. Most of the roughly fourteen thousand residents had left— not because of the warning pamphlets the Israeli planes had dropped the day before, but because we had told them what we planned to do. Now the town was eerily silent. No donkeys brayed in their pens; not an infant whimpered for its mother. Nobody could see our seven thousand or so Fatah fighters hidden behind stone walls or under tarpaulins, amid date trees and olive groves—a reception committee waiting to roll out a blood red carpet for the invaders.

3

A trained sniper at seventeen years old, I stood ready to do my job, waiting up on the hill for the opportune moment. I would pick off any IDF machine gunner who dared to stick his head up out of a tank or jeep. A soft breeze moved through the grass. I stared intently at the Allenby Bridge in the distance, the main crossing from the Israeli-controlled West Bank to the Jordanian territory where we sat.

Sure enough, the first vehicles in the convoy now came into view, their camouflage colors making them difficult to detect. This was the same IDF that had so humiliated the Arab armies nine months before in the infamous Six-Day War. We Palestinians had been peppering them ever since with hit-and-run attacks—a grenade here, a three-minute skirmish there. Now they had decided to storm our training camp at al-Karameh in force. They wanted to take out our operation wholesale, and maybe even get our heroic leader "Abu Ammar"—Yasser Arafat—in the process.

A trained sniper at seventeen years old, I stood ready to do my job.

They figured most of us guerrilla fighters would have pulled back and away from the showdown, like so many times before. They had no idea that the wily Arafat had switched strategies this time, saying to us, "We will make a stand in this place. We will fight with honor. The whole of the Arab people are watching us. We will crush the myth that the IDF is invincible!"

And they certainly did not expect the newest tactic we would use today for the very first time: suicide bombers. We had gotten volunteers who were willing to make this their final battle for Palestinian justice. They now waited on rooftops in their bulky vests loaded with explosives until the moment came to jump into the streets below.

DEADLY SURPRISE

The growling of the IDF engines grew louder. My heart began to pound. I positioned myself for steady action as I peered through my scope. The enemy convoy reached the edge of the town. I picked out my closest target, trained the weapon on his head, and ever so carefully squeezed the Simonov's trigger.

At nearly the same moment, my comrades below began firing from their hiding places. The firefight exploded all at once. The noise was deafening. At that time, the Israeli infantry had no flak jackets, so we were able to wound or kill them right away. All hell broke loose that morning in al-Karameh.

Of course, we began taking our own casualties, too. Every Fatah fighter knew that would happen. None of us counted on surviving the day. We were fully prepared to die. We might never see the moon again, but we would regain our honor. That was, in fact, the meaning of this town's name, *Karameh*. It was the Arabic word for "honor" or "dignity."

The street battle raged on at full force while I kept picking off targets from the hillside. Minutes passed, perhaps even a full hour. There was no subtlety to our approach; we were going with every thrust we had to inflict mortal damage on the Jews. Then a massive bomb blast shook the entire valley. Our troops had blown up the Allenby Bridge, cutting off the escape route if the IDF tried to pull back. The Israelis were now trapped on our side of the Jordan— the east side—and would have to fight to the death. Only a miracle of Joshua-at-Jericho–sized proportions would save them now.

> We might never see the moon again, but we would regain our honor.

A few minutes later, my commander shouted at me with alarm in his voice: "Do you hear that? Helicopter gunships are coming!" I had been too focused on my targets to notice. "Get off this hill!" he ordered. "If you stay here, they'll blow you to bits from the air! Get down into the town with everybody else!"

I scrambled down the hill to join my comrades in the fight. There the conflict grew increasingly close range. There was hardly room to use a weapon. It became a hand-to-hand brawl with fists, knives, and even rocks. We put our karate and judo training to use immediately. The two sides were so intermingled that their helicopter gunners couldn't sort us out. At that point, I was fighting on sheer instinct. There was no time to think or strategize. I simply kept bashing the nearest IDF soldier before he could bash me.

I could tell the enemy was bewildered by our bravery. They had expected us to act more like classic guerrilla fighters, feinting and withdrawing. Instead, here we were in a no-holds-barred fracas. Guys were screaming, blood was splashing, the wounded were moaning, and all of us were jumping over an increasing number of dead bodies to keep up the attack. I glanced down at several cuts on my arm but paid little attention. The kick of adrenaline was too strong for me to worry about injuries.

We Fatah fighters were in fact more agile than the IDF since we carried less gear than they did and could therefore run faster. We also had our bayonets already fixed on our weapons and ready to use while the Israelis were still fumbling to get theirs off their belts and attached. At times they literally ran into our knives.

Whenever they tried to regroup behind one of their tanks, a suicide bomber would leap down from a rooftop with a thunderous explosion of nails and other metal bits. Blood spattered, and body parts flew through the air.

Occasionally throughout the afternoon, there would be a short lull in the fighting while the Israelis barricaded themselves inside a house. We would then quickly set up in the house across the street, from which we would open fire again. We stormed building after building.

BRAGGING RIGHTS

Somehow, after seven hours of gruesome combat, a ceasefire was called. I still do not know who arranged that or how it was done. The IDF withdrew and headed downriver to find another bridge they could use for returning to the West Bank. The smoke over al-Karameh began to clear. "We won! We won!" we shouted, slapping each other on the back. "We stood up to the Jews and beat them!"

We danced around the four IDF tanks we had destroyed, along with three half-tracks, two armored jeeps, and even one airplane. The symbolism for us was huge. We had done what the regular Arab armies had failed to do three times: in 1948, 1956, and the previous year. We would be featured the next day in the world's headlines. We had shown that we Palestinians were no longer just a pitiful clump of refugees. We were a proud and courageous people who had been robbed of our homeland and were on the march to take it back.

I was especially thrilled to commandeer a Willys Jeep that the Israelis had left behind. A vehicle of my own! I invited some of my comrades to jump in for a quick drive through the town.

As evening approached, we turned our attention to counting our losses. My unit of eight now numbered only three. Across the town, we went about the somber task of gathering and burying the dead. We mourned the fact that these friends were gone forever. It hurt deep within our souls, and we swore we would avenge them.

The longer we worked, the more we realized we had paid a high price on that day. We eventually tallied 128 dead, several dozen wounded, and 150 missing. These numbers, we had to admit, were probably greater than the losses suffered by the IDF.

But it was all worth it, we told ourselves. The Israelis had come from Jericho, looking for a fight, and we had given them far more than they had ever expected. Our cause was now catapulted to a whole new level.

More than anything, we could hold our heads high in the presence of the man in a checkered headdress who had watched the entire battle from a hilltop not far from where I had begun the day. He had seen our bravery, our determination, our sacrifice. The Israelis had wanted desperately to find him that day and kill him, but they had failed. His leadership stood intact. Yasser Arafat was alive and well, and we revered him more than ever.

CHAPTER 2

THE
MAKING
OF
A
TROUBLEMAKER

I WOULD BE THE FIRST TO ADMIT that, in the United States at least, we Palestinians would not win a popularity contest anytime soon. We are viewed as the world's troublemakers. We're known for lobbing rockets into quiet Israeli neighborhoods, recruiting suicide bombers to blow up buses and restaurants, frustrating the best-laid peace plans, and complaining about daily restrictions in the Gaza Strip and West Bank. One respected research firm in 2006 measured American sympathies at 52 percent for Israel, 11 percent for Palestinians. Those numbers have stayed roughly the same for forty years, ever since the Six-Day War.[1]

No one person can speak for—or explain—all eleven million Palestinians scattered across the world. As for me, I admit I stirred up plenty of trouble in my early years. The resentment that lodged within my soul at a young age found its release in schoolyard fights, family arguments, scrapes with the police—and finally, at not quite seventeen, in running away from home to join Fatah, a Palestinian nationalist party and eventual member of the multi-party Palestine Liberation Organization (PLO). There I was trained as a sniper, waiting in the shadows to pick off unsuspecting lives. Even when I moved to America at age twenty-three, the rage inside me burned on. How that fire was finally quenched is this book's story.

I was born in a tent in the squalid al-Breij refugee camp of Gaza City in early 1951, the third child of a former orange grove manager and his wife from Jaffa. Three years before, when the state of Israel was declared, their comfortable life had been turned upside down by the order to move. "Step aside," the Arab governments of Jordan, Syria, and Egypt said, in effect. "Get out of the way so our armies can move in and drive these crazy Zionists into the sea."

My father's business partner, a Jew, had offered his protection and counseled him not to act hastily. He assured my father that leaving wasn't necessary, that they could keep the business going together. But the safer choice, my parents believed, was to move to the sidelines of the battlefield and hope for an early return once the fighting ended.

> We Palestinians would not win a popularity contest anytime soon.

The 1948 war, however, did not go as predicted by the politicians in Cairo, Amman, and Damascus. In fact, the day in mid-May that Israelis now celebrate as Independence Day turned into what my people still call *al-Nakba* ("the catastrophe" in Arabic). Some seven hundred thousand Palestinians were displaced; more than four hundred Arab-majority villages were destroyed or abandoned. The words of Great Britain's famous Balfour Declaration of 1917, favoring a national home for the Jewish people *so long as* "nothing shall be done which may prejudice the civil and religious rights of existing non-Jewish communities in Palestine," had turned to smoke and ashes.

By 1951 the Saada family had endured three winters in the tent, with overnight temperatures sometimes dipping as low as forty degrees Fahrenheit. Would we ever go home again? Not a sliver of hope appeared. One day my father stared across the muddy landscape and realized that the ultimate Arab indignity had fallen upon him: *no land.* In the Arab culture, no land equals no honor. All his dreams had crumbled.

OFF TO A FARAWAY PLACE

I was only two months old, my mother having just recovered from giving birth, when the United Nations authorities squeezed our family of five onto an overcrowded freighter to head for a new and unfamiliar place where we might start over. We sailed through the Suez Canal and down the Red Sea, nine hundred miles in all, to the desolate seaport city of Jiddah, Saudi Arabia. My earliest memories are of this place, with sand everywhere, electricity only at rare intervals, and summer heat so oppressive we slept on the roof. But at least we had a modest house here instead of a tent. It was made of brick and had three bedrooms. Here I learned to walk and talk; I'm told I still carry a slight Saudi accent in my speech.

My grandmother, uncles, and other relatives had come along on the same ship. In time, the men worked together to open a small garage since my father was good at auto-body repair and my uncles were good at mechanics. In fact, my father had worked for the British Royal Air Force back in happier days, repairing fuselages on their legendary Spitfire fighter planes. Now he applied his knowledge to fenders and bumpers, eventually even getting business from King Saud, who had a fleet of fancy vehicles. In those days, Jiddah was the diplomatic hub of the country, with many embassies and government offices.

Although the money for our family was an improvement in this new land, the welcome from its native Saudis was not. They bluntly called us "refugees" and "immigrants" to our faces. I realized quickly, even before starting school, that we were not wanted here. In our Western-style trousers and shirts, we stood out to the Saudis, who wore long robes. We heard the blatantly false accusation that we had *sold* our land—our honor—back in Palestine to the Jews, just to make money, and that now we had come here looking to take over Saudi land. Nothing could have been further from the truth.

The local flavor of Islam, called Wahhabism, was also a shock. We considered ourselves Muslim, but we were not nearly as strict as these Muslims. One day, my father was trying to finish up a job on a car of the king, who wanted it back soon. In order to meet the request, my father was working in the garage on Friday, the holy day of Islam. The door, unfortunately, was ajar.

I was with him there, watching as he tried to finish. Noontime came. The mournful chant sounded from the minaret of the nearby mosque, calling the faithful to prayer. My father kept working.

Suddenly a squadron of *mutawwa*—religious police—came thundering into the garage. "Infidel!" they screamed. They attacked him with a whip as they shouted, "Why are you working instead of praying? You refugees show no respect! Go to the mosque this very minute!" They chased him outside and down the street, whipping him repeatedly with sharp blows. I heard him cry out in pain as he ran toward the mosque.

> Suddenly a squadron of *mutawwa* came thundering into the garage. "Infidel!" they screamed.

I could not believe what was happening. Though only seven years old, I tried to intervene. I pulled on the robe of the man who was pursuing my father. "Don't beat him! Stop it!" I cried, but it did no good.

I still remember how exhausted he looked staggering home after mosque prayers had concluded. My mother bandaged his wounds. I was still crying. How could they do such a thing to an honest worker like my dad? Didn't his connections to the king count for something?

We had come to this country thinking we were good Muslims. My grandmother even took me on some Fridays to Mecca, fifty miles inland, for prayers. A relative of ours drove a taxi; he would pick us up at three o'clock in the morning in order to arrive on time for the 4:40 service in the Grand Mosque around the sacred Kaaba, surrounded by a crowd of reverent worshipers. I loved those trips.

Our family celebrated all the Muslim feasts. Our parents fasted during the holy month of Ramadan. But now these men had beaten my father in the name of Islam. I couldn't understand it.

BATTLE ROYAL

When it came to dealing with those my own age, I learned quickly to use my fists. Many of the local children were Bedouin and didn't go to school at all, moving frequently from place to place with their camels. On the other hand, some were members of the large royal family, so at school I found myself sitting alongside a number of princes. They didn't intimidate me. I was just as willing to pick a fight with a prince as with anyone else.

The teachers set a climate of intimidation, letting us immigrant kids know we were not appreciated. I admit I was a difficult child; I cheated and even forced others to do my homework. I often had to put my hand on the teacher's desk to receive the whack of the ruler for something I'd done. But the inequities of discipline made me all the angrier.

One day in second grade, my Palestinian friends and I were playing soccer with a stone, since we didn't have a proper ball. Along came one of the princes with his Lebanese and Syrian followers to thrash us. Before I knew what had happened, the prince had thrown me to the ground. But my friends jumped to my aid, and soon we came surging back. I pounded the prince in the face and stomach.

Of course, the screaming drew the teachers' attention. Soon we were all sitting in the principal's office. He reprimanded us all—then made us Palestinians lie down on the floor so he could beat the bare soles of our feet with a whip. The Saudi kids got away with nothing. The school officials were afraid of their family connections.

When the prince arrived home that day with scratches all over his face, his father wanted to know what had happened. Upon hearing his son's version of the story, the angry father summoned my father for an explanation. Soon he whipped off his headscarf holder, twisted it into a tight rope, and began beating my father with it. "If your son touches the prince one more time, your whole family will be dead!" he threatened.

My father came home exasperated. Using my formal name, he

lectured, "Taysir, you must stop getting us into trouble! Stop the fighting! You're going to kill us all!" When he finally calmed down, he added, "I insist that you respect the people of this country. They have taken us in. Even when they beat us, we must bear it without revolting against them. We must remain calm."

I didn't agree with that viewpoint at all—especially in light of how much we Palestinians were doing for the country. We had more education and job skills than many Saudis at that time. We were helping build up the nation. We were cleaner and more organized. Behind nearly every government minister stood a Palestinian aide who made his department look good. Why should we be harassed and insulted?

> "Even when they beat us, we must bear it without revolting against them."

But I kept silent. If only we could go back to Palestine. If only the Jews hadn't stolen our land. . . .

The imams who taught our religion classes at school railed against them. "The Jews have rejected Allah. They are apes and pigs—it says so right here in the Qur'an. Allah is calling us now to eliminate them. If we don't, they will come here to Saudi Arabia and overrun our country, too." Hatred was building up in my young heart.

My father, I must say, did not share my disgust. He told us stories of past relationships with Jews, before 1948, that were harmonious. He didn't complain about the daily trials of being a refugee. He didn't bemoan the multiple times he was thrown in jail for this infraction or that. The fact that even a street sweeper could insult him and he wasn't allowed to say anything in reply did not seem to upset him. I, on the other hand, was incensed by all of this.

BIN LADEN TALES

The remarkable thing was that my father could even find occasional humor in the events of his life. He told us stories about the wealthy contractor who seemed to control most of the big building projects in the country. He had come from Yemen, at the far southern tip of the Arabian Peninsula, and had worked his way up from a lowly dockhand in the port to his present summit of power. He often brought his cars to our garage for repair. His name was Muhammad bin Laden.

"Do you want to hear why he is so rich?" my father asked one evening with a chuckle. I remember well his explanation: "Several years ago, the Ministry of Religious Affairs placed a big order with his company for hand fans to give the pilgrims." Jiddah was the port through which hundreds of thousands of Muslims entered the country each year for *hajj*, the sacred pilgrimage to Mecca.

"They ordered fifty thousand fans. The bin Ladens imported them from a factory in Sudan and charged the government five ghirsh apiece. But the invoice got misplaced somehow, and the bill was never paid. Muhammad bin Laden didn't press the issue.

"Then just recently, the same government department ordered five thousand *electric* fans, which cost five riyals each." (At that time one riyal equaled twenty-two ghirsh.) "When they got ready to pay the second bill, they stumbled across the first bill, too—but it was blurry from some water that had been spilled on it. They couldn't read the prices on the first bill. So they just assumed that all the fans were alike on both deliveries. They paid this man for all the fans at five riyals each! And he didn't say a word about the mistake. Maybe he just said to himself, 'It is the will of Allah.'"

Another story had to do with the construction of a new palace for King Saud. A team of British engineers warned the king that bin Laden's work was unstable, and the roof would likely collapse. The king called in his contractor for a meeting.

"Here is what the engineers are saying," he told bin Laden. "Is it true that your building will fall down on my head?"

Bin Laden, a wiry little man, only smiled. "Your Highness," he said at last, "please give me three days. Then I will show you something."

Three days later, the king and his entourage, including the engineers, arrived at the construction site. They were astonished to see a massive earthen ramp on one side leading up to the palace roof.

Muhammad bin Laden arrived just then at the wheel of a large Mack truck loaded with stone. Waving to the king, he revved the engine and drove the truck straight up the ramp and onto the roof. He then got out of the cab to jump up and down on the structure.

"Does Your Highness really believe that this roof is going to come down?" he shouted.

The watching crowd of dignitaries broke into laughter, all except the engineers. King Saud was clearly amused. When bin Laden returned to ground level, the king motioned to his treasurer and said, "Take his truck. Load it up with silver riyals—and then give it back to him." The British engineers were promptly thrown out of the country.

My father concluded, "We've all heard the saying about somebody being worth their weight in gold. I guess the king considers this man to be worth his *truck's* weight in silver!"

I remember being at my father's garage one day when Muhammad bin Laden stopped by with a car needing repair. He happened to bring along a small boy, one of his many sons, who was five or six years younger than me. He didn't attend my school. He seemed very shy and kept to himself while our two fathers did business together.

I did find out the son's name that day, however. The entire world would learn it many years later. It was Osama.

THE PRINCE AND HIS SPORTS CAR

When I was ten years old, my father faced perhaps his greatest challenge at the garage. It was the time of the hajj, and a nephew of the sheik who ruled Qatar decided to make the journey from his country over on the Persian Gulf. Instead of flying, he got the idea to drive his sporty Oldsmobile Cutlass Supreme across the Arabian desert. On the way, he had a serious accident, rolling his car, but fortunately, he survived.

Once his attendants got him to Jiddah, he, of course, told King Saud about his misfortune. "I love that car!" he moaned. "I don't know what to do now."

"Don't worry," said the king. "I have a garage here that does amazing body work. I'm sure they will be able to restore your car like new."

My father was given directions on where to find the car out in the desert. As soon as he saw it, he knew the restoration work would cost more than the car was worth. In fact, it might even be impossible.

"Your Highness," he reported back to King Saud, "the car has been completely destroyed. It would be far better to buy a new one. This car really is a total loss."

The Qatari prince, however, would not listen. "No, I love this car! Repair it! I don't care how much it costs!"

The king only looked in my father's direction and said, "Give it a try. See what you can do."

With a sigh, my father went to work. He spent ten days attempting to undo the damage. When he took it back to the palace, the prince was ecstatic. "Excellent job!" he exclaimed. "If it wasn't for the cigarette burn on the front seat, I wouldn't believe it was the same car. This is marvelous!"

And then came the words nobody expected: "I want you to come with me to Qatar and take care of all my cars!"

"Oh, no; we are happy here," my father replied. "King Saud is very kind to us. I have eight children now. My family and I have a good life here in Jiddah."

The king looked at my father and uttered one simple, declarative sentence.

"You have permission to go with him."

This meant we had no option. The "permission" was really an order. Just like that, in a matter of seconds, the ruler had spoken, and an entire family's life was uprooted once again.

When I heard about it, I was furious. What were we—little pawns on a royal chessboard, to be pushed about at will? Why did King Saud do such a terrible thing? My father's business was thriving. Even though I didn't feel at home in Saudi Arabia, I at least had a few friends. My life was about to be destroyed.

First they humiliate us by calling us "refugees," I said to myself. Now they're turning us into gypsies. Why can't they leave us alone?

A few days later, my father was loading our belongings into the truck for our move eight hundred miles east. I was crying, even raging. Behind his back I began unloading the truck, putting luggage and boxes back out onto the ground again. The resentment was boiling up in my chest.

In a matter of seconds the ruler had spoken, and an entire family's life was uprooted once again.

My father watched me with sad, empty eyes. He then pushed me aside without speaking and loaded the items back into their places. I kept unloading until he said, "Taysir, stop it! None of us wants to go. But we have to obey." He was resigned to his fate. I finally acquiesced, not wanting to make this great man suffer even more.

Our chances of ever getting back to green, well-watered Palestine were now even less likely. It simply wasn't fair.

CHAPTER 3

A CAUSE
WORTH
FIGHTING
FOR

WHEN WE ARRIVED IN DOHA, the capital city of Qatar, it was just as sandy as Jiddah had been—and even hotter. One saving grace was that we again had a nearby beach for cooling off, only this time on the Persian Gulf instead of the Red Sea. My family and I would love going there to dive in the salty waves.

I noticed right away that the Qataris were friendlier to our family. Nobody scorned us as refugees. The whole country seemed more relaxed, with only seventy-five thousand people living on this peninsula a hundred miles long and fifty miles wide. Many were Bedouins, who moved frequently throughout the land. The oil bonanza was just beginning in those days; we never in our wildest dreams imagined what Qatar would become today—the third-richest nation per capita on earth and home to the media powerhouse Al Jazeera.

My father and my uncles got busy opening three garages at once, as Prince Abdul Rahman wanted. One was for mechanical work, the next for electrical jobs, and the third for body work. Success came quickly. The young prince became our family's best friend, stopping often at our house to play with us kids or share a meal. If it happened to be the middle of the day, he would stretch out on the floor to nap, just as we did. He was a down-to-earth man in spite of his wealth, wearing ordinary clothes in the street and even taking food to the poor who needed it. We Palestinians loved him.

It's a good thing he liked us, because my aggressive streak necessitated the help of a friend in high places more than once, especially as I moved into my teenage years. An uncle taught me how to drive as soon as I was tall enough to see over the dashboard. I'd go racing through the capital, passing other cars whether it was safe or not. It wasn't long before I got pulled over by the police.

"How old are you, son?" the officer asked.

"Thirteen."

"That is definitely too young to drive!" he announced. He made me get into his vehicle for a quick trip to the police station, while another officer followed in my car.

They called my father, who promptly notified Prince Rahman. Soon both of them walked in. "What do you think you're doing with this young man?" the prince stormed at the officer in charge. "Did he do anything wrong? Quit harassing him!" He pulled off his turban and folded it into a whip as he ordered the officer, "Step outside with me!"

Out in the parking lot, he proceeded to whip the officer. When he finished, he said, "Now, drive this young man's car home for him. And don't let me catch you doing this kind of thing again!" I tried to suppress my smile at this turn of events.

That was not my last visit to the police station, however. Qatar, a British protectorate until 1971, naturally saw the presence of British officials. It irritated me that the British diplomats and business people had marked off a section of the beach just for themselves. No Arabs were allowed there.

Oh, really? I began swimming under the fence they had built, holding my breath until I could get close enough to pinch a toe or a leg underwater. They would go screaming toward the sand. "Get out of the water! There's a big fish out there that just bit me!" About this time, I would come up for air and laugh at the pandemonium I had caused.

Soon the British came prepared with goggles to chase me in the water, and I was hauled ashore and turned over to the police. The chief knew better than to mess with me, though. He didn't want a repeat encounter with Prince Rahman. He simply called my father and complained.

When my dad picked me up and got me home, he personally took on the chore of whipping me with a hose. "You never stop stirring up trouble for us!" he shouted. "One day we're all going to get thrown out of the country because of you!" I don't remember very many times when my father became truly angry, but this was one of them.

Meanwhile, Prince Rahman heard parts and pieces of the story—enough to send him racing down to the police station again. He began accusing the poor police chief of beating me. But then my father showed up to set the record straight. "Rahman, please stop. This man did not beat my son; he didn't even touch him. I'm the one who disciplined him this time." The prince calmed down.

It was a tragic day for us when Prince Rahman got into a feud with another sheik and his family. A fight broke out, and Rahman shot one of his adversaries, killing him. He then knew he would have to turn himself in to the authorities. He did so voluntarily.

The sentence for this act was death, but he was so popular that none of the Qatari authorities would carry out the execution. The family of the other sheik kept pressing for justice. Finally they managed to get the British chief of police to do the deed. He walked into Prince Rahman's prison cell one day, shot him in the head, and immediately dashed to the airport to leave the country. Our friend and protector would assist us no more. We mourned the loss.

> The chief knew better than to mess with me. He didn't want a repeat encounter with Prince Rahman.

DAREDEVIL ON WHEELS

In school I was obnoxious, standing up in the middle of class to voice my displeasure if the teacher had crossed me. My grades were poor, in spite of the papers I turned in that were written by other students whom I had coerced. The teachers hesitated to confront me or to alarm my parents. I simply didn't care.

I was more interested in fantasizing about girls, who went to a separate school from us boys. My friends and I would park outside their school at the end of the day and wave to them, trying to get their attention. Any closer attention in a Muslim society would have been foolhardy, and we knew not to press too hard. We tried to think of sly ways to get their phone numbers. But even that was risky—what if another family member answered instead?

One afternoon I challenged a prince to a race. My Dodge had a big engine, and I was sure I could beat him, even in his new Mercedes. We taunted each other about how we would humiliate the other. Then we started down a two-lane asphalt road outside of town, side by side. Faster and faster we went.

And then the inevitable happened: A car was coming the opposite way . . . in my lane. I glanced at the prince to see if he would pull to the side and give me space. He kept roaring straight ahead. The oncoming car was now less than a hundred feet in front of me. There wasn't enough time to slow down and pull in behind the prince. I was doomed!

I pulled the steering wheel hard to the outside and skidded into the sand as the approaching car zoomed past me. I went into a vicious spin that threw me out of the vehicle altogether. My car rolled over several times and finally came to rest on the hot desert, utterly demolished.

The next thing I remember is people running to see how badly I was hurt. "Are you still alive?" the prince gasped. Actually, I had suffered only a few scrapes. Everyone was amazed at how fortunate I had been.

The prince then drove me back to Doha. My other piece of good fortune was that my father was away in Germany just then on a business trip to the Mercedes plant. That evening, I borrowed my uncle's car, and the prince and I headed back out to the crash site. I still needed to show him which one of us was faster. Well, *I* was—faster in causing another wreck, that is. I lost control of the car and slammed into a street lamp, resulting in major damage. We quietly drove back to park the car outside my uncle's house and then slinked away.

The next day when it was time for me to pick up my younger brothers and sisters from school, I said to my mother, "I need to use Dad's car today. Mine is in the shop being repaired." She innocently handed me the keys to his big, old Chrysler Imperial, a real battleship.

Soon I was cruising around Doha with no destination in mind. I turned a corner and ended up somehow in the wrong lane. Another car was bearing down on me, and when we collided, there was a huge bang. The big Chrysler was badly damaged. I had just crashed my third car in two days.

When Dad returned from Germany, he was understandably upset. "No more cars for you!" he exclaimed. "From now on, you will either walk or take the school bus."

I would rather have died than ride the school bus. I quickly began lining up friends to pick me up whenever I wanted to go somewhere. And before long, one of my younger uncles gave me another car, anyway.

But this was not the car I really wanted. I got a job that spring of 1967 with a Datsun dealer, a friend of my father's, as a car salesman. I was only sixteen years old, but I could work every day after school and into the evening.

I had just crashed my third car in two days.

The sleek Datsun 200Z, a sports car that made us all drool, had just come on the market then. I said to the dealer, "If you'll give me one of those, I will sell twenty-four more in the first month!"

He eyed me suspiciously. Then a grin came over his face. "From what I've heard about your driving, I shouldn't." He paused.

"But all right—I'll take up your proposal. Show me what you can do."

I was never happier than the day I first drove up and down the main street of Doha in my very own light blue 200Z. I proceeded slowly so everyone would have time to gaze upon this marvelous, arrow-shaped masterpiece. Then I went to my uncle's garage to dress it up even more with white racing stripes and other enhancements. This was *my* car, *my* baby. I loved this piece of machinery as much as, in a few years, I would come to love my assault rifle. It was my personal statement of daring adventure.

I even got a photographer to take pictures of me shooting off a bump and into the air at 160 kilometers per hour—100 mph. It made a fantastic photo, which was marketed throughout the country. Soon the backlog of orders for the 200Z was two months long. The dealer was very pleased, of course. He even sent me on a trip to visit the Datsun headquarters in Japan and learn more about selling the car. And I was still a teenager!

A NEW VOICE

But when I was by myself, with no audience to impress, I had to admit my life felt empty. What were we all doing in Qatar, anyway? This was not the land of my fathers. I felt no affinity for this place. Why couldn't the mighty Arab people rise up and get control of my homeland once again? We had lost two wars already—the initial one in 1948, and the war in 1956. This was ridiculous. If the Jews didn't have the aid of their rich Christian friends in Britain and America, I thought, we would have sacked them long ago.

We had the superior religion; of that I was sure. Judaism and Christianity were from distant history; Islam had come along more recently to fix the problems and misunderstandings of them both. Allah would surely bring us victory in the next conflict, which couldn't be far away. I could hardly wait for Palestine to be liberated.

It was around this time that my school friends and I started hearing about a new voice in this dilemma. He was a Palestinian like us, although he had grown up and gone to college in Cairo, Egypt, and had become a civil engineer. He had fought the Israelis around Gaza in 1948 and more recently had founded, with two friends, the Palestine National Liberation Movement. The Arabic name for the group could be condensed down to the acronym *HaTaF*, but that word—meaning "sudden death"—was obviously a bad choice. So this man had reversed the letters to come up with *FaTaH*, which in Arabic means "the opener."

> Why couldn't the mighty Arab people rise up and get control of my homeland once again?

His name was Yasser Arafat.

"The Arab governments are never going to get our land back," he said. "They talk a good game, but they don't produce. They have already tried twice and been humiliated both times. They make promises they cannot keep—or don't even intend to keep when they make them.

"The only way forward in reclaiming our homeland is for us Palestinians to take matters into our own hands," Arafat insisted. "We are the ones who must do this. After all, we are the ones who are suffering as refugees all over the Middle East and even beyond. We are the ones whose honor has been disgraced. We must look to no one but ourselves to rise up and cast out the Jewish intruders!"

My friends and I were swept up by this man's charisma. When I saw him on television, I had never heard anyone who so clearly pierced through the fog of politics and called the facts what they were. I fully agreed—the years were passing by with no results. Hopes and wishes were not going to get the job done. We Palestinians would have to seize our own destiny. We had the motivation to stand up and fight for our very existence as a people. No one else felt our pain deeply enough to care.

This marvelous man became our hero. Here was someone who could have made a comfortable life for himself in the oil industry, but instead he was risking everything for a battle worth waging. We would help him fight!

Arafat lived in Kuwait, but he frequently came to Qatar to raise funds. Whenever he did, my father would write him a check. I began to wonder if there was anything I could do to help. Surely Fatah needed courageous young fighters to press the battle. I was almost done with high school. A fantasy filled my mind: driving my beloved Datsun 200Z down the streets of Gaza or Jerusalem someday. Wouldn't that be a thrill!

WAR AT LAST

Then came a surprise. On June 5, 1967, Israel attacked Egypt's air force. Egypt, Jordan, Syria, and other forces struck back. The war was on. We sat glued to our radios awaiting the glorious victory. I got out a piece of paper and began writing down how many Israeli planes our side had shot down. In the first four days, I counted 720 aircraft brought down by our brave Arab pilots and antiaircraft brigades. Yes!

"How many planes do they have, anyway?" I asked my father. "We've already shot down 720 of them. They can't have many more left." He didn't know the answer, but he was as confident as I that a wonderful triumph was underway. We would soon return! *Palestine, here we come!*

We heard nothing on the radio about Arab casualties. It seemed that our forces were steamrolling the Jews. This would no doubt be a short and decisive war.

And then, on June 11, came the greatest shock imaginable. The Arab armies had laid down their weapons and agreed to a ceasefire. Israel was now in control of the Gaza Strip, the entire Sinai Peninsula, the West Bank (including East Jerusalem), and the Golan Heights up north. Their territory had just multiplied three times! There had obviously been no great loss of Israeli warplanes. Instead, "The Six-Day War," as it was now being called, had devastated Arab armaments—and Arab pride.

I simply could not believe it! I jumped into my car that night and drove around Doha for hours, cursing the media that had lied to us, railing against the stupidity of it all. I was furious that once again we had lost to Israel. How could this be? With all our soldiers and weapons and oil money, how could that handful of people in that little country beat us? What a terrible embarrassment! Something was definitely wrong. The resentment I had sustained all my life took a quantum leap upward.

The thought never crossed my teenage mind that at that moment, the Jews and their Christian friends might be saying to themselves, "See, God was on our side. He helped us against overwhelming odds." If I had conceived of such an explanation, I would have been even more irate. *So, what about us?* I would have flung back toward heaven. *Don't we Palestinians count for anything? Do you care that we keep getting pushed away from our home? Where is the fairness in that?!*

Two weeks later, Yasser Arafat was back in Qatar. He actually came to our house for a reception that my parents arranged. Dressed in a military uniform, he was in his thirties and wore a black-and-white checked *kaffiyeh* headdress.

"Do you now see what I mean when I have been saying we must fight our own battles?" he said to the crowd as heads nodded all over the room. I was mesmerized in the man's presence. As the evening went on, I kept edging closer until I finally managed to sit next to him.

"Once again, the Arab governments have proven how impotent they are. Once again, they have been shamed by the Zionists and their allies. Neither the Saudis nor the Jordanians, neither the Syrians nor the Egyptians have the will to take back our land. They have in fact gotten us into a worse position now than before. We can count on no one but ourselves."

He is exactly right, I said to myself.

TIME FOR MORE THAN WORDS

This call to arms churned within me day and night. In a few months, after another one of my aimless, agitated rides in my car, I returned home and approached my father. "Dad," I began, "the time has come for you to sacrifice at least one of your sons to the cause. We cannot go on living like this. A Bedouin rules over us! We are being exploited here. Nobody really accepts us. We will never be secure and prosperous until we reclaim our land by force."

He looked at me, waiting for my next sentence.

"It is time," I announced with all seriousness, "for me to join Arafat's movement!"

My father took a moment to compose his thoughts, then said, "Son, you are still in school. Finish your education, just as your brother is doing now. Then you can think about war.

"You are right: Every family has to give somebody. I agree with you on that. We, too, will give—but not just now. We are giving a lot of money to this cause, as I think you know. At the moment, there are enough people willing to fight. Once you have finished your education, you can serve the cause in a better way."

Our conversation ended in a stalemate. I did not argue with him. But in my heart, I knew that delay was not an option for me. Soon I was talking with two friends who wanted to join Fatah as strongly as I did. We simply could not sit around waiting for someone else to do the job we were meant to do.

> We simply could not sit around waiting for someone else to do the job we were meant to do.

"All right," one of us said at last, "let's leave the country on a 'vacation.' We can buy our tickets and go to Damascus, where the Fatah headquarters are, without anyone's permission."

"But what about the exit visa?" someone asked. "We aren't old enough to sign for ourselves."

"We will get the documents from the Ministry of the Interior and forge our fathers' signatures."

And that is what happened in November of that year, 1967. We packed our belongings in secret, and another friend from school drove us to the airport. We flew out of Qatar without saying goodbye to anyone. Our personal jihad had begun.

CHAPTER 4

GROWING UP FAST

I WAS NERVOUS WALKING UP TO THE FATAH BUILDING on the outskirts of Damascus, especially as I saw more and more guards and barbed wire. I thought to myself that even the ruler's palace back in Qatar didn't have this much protection.

The gatekeeper was a tall, thin, mean-looking man in fatigues who hadn't shaved in several days. He gave us a curt nod as he took the cigarette out of his mouth and waited for us to explain ourselves.

"We have come from Qatar," I said hesitantly. "We want to fight for the Palestinian people. We want to join Fatah."

He gave us another long, suspicious look. After all, he had to be on guard against spies. But we looked too naive for that, and so he spoke at last. "All right. Go through that second door over there and find the recruitment office." As soon as we were past his checkpoint, I looked at my two friends and faintly smiled. We had at least passed the first hurdle on our quest.

The designated office had little furniture. A clerk asked us what we wanted. We gave the same explanation as before. Soon we were sent to a dusty, paper-laden desk where a young man sat close to an overflowing ashtray. "What do you want?" he inquired.

For the third time we told of our wish to fight for the Palestinian homeland. The longer we talked, the more I could tell he had heard this kind of tale many times. He was used to dealing with idealistic teenage boys.

"Where are you from?" he said, looking in my direction.

"From Qatar—but my family had a business in Jaffa. They had to flee in 1948, so I was born in Gaza. That's why I want to join Fatah—to free Palestine!" My enthusiasm got a little overheated at that point.

The man nodded quietly, then asked my friends about their roots. Both of them named cities in the West Bank but then added that they had grown up in Qatar.

He asked several more questions. He did not ask, however, if we had our parents' permission to be here. We were glad about that. Perhaps he didn't care, since Fatah needed all the troops it could get.

After an hour or so, we were put onto a small, rickety bus for an unknown destination. We rode through the busy streets of Damascus, staring out the windows at this city—huge to our eyes, with more than half a million residents. The traffic was noisy, the markets colorful. This was the biggest metropolis any of us had ever seen.

Then we were out in the countryside again, until we arrived at Fatah's induction compound. A large green tent occupied the center of the area, surrounded by row upon row of smaller beige tents with pointed roofs for two to four recruits each. After some preliminary processing, we were assigned to tents, separated from one another. There would be no more idle camaraderie among the three of us. From now on, it was all business.

The next morning, I was handed a pad of paper and a pen. "Start writing your life story," the officer ordered. "Tell everything you've ever done, everything that has been done to you. We want all the details. Don't leave anything out." This was my job for the day . . . and the next . . . and the next. I figured out that Fatah was screening me to look for any flaw or hint that might disqualify me. The risk of my being a spy for Israel or the CIA or some other country had to be ruled out.

Among other things, the supervisors wanted to know my full name.

"I'd rather not say," I replied.

"Why not?"

"Well, my parents don't exactly know I'm here. It wouldn't be good to tell them."

"We will not tell them—we promise you," they replied. "But you have to tell us your name. Otherwise, we can't use you."

Reluctantly I confessed my name, hoping against hope that word would not get back to Qatar. Once that was settled, I was given my new identity. From now on in Fatah, I would be known as *Jazzar*— "Butcher." I liked that. These people understood me!

After ten days in this compound, a large group of us recruits was loaded into the back of a van with no windows. "Now you will go for training," the officer said, without giving any more detail. We rode for hours and hours. The van grew more humid and we grew more sweaty as the time passed. Our group was strangely quiet as we rumbled down the road.

We crossed the border from Syria into Jordan. Finally, with stiff joints we stepped out into the sunshine again, in the middle of a forest. We saw a couple of buildings, many tents, and once again security fences all around the perimeter, with plenty of guards. The smell of earth and trees was wonderfully refreshing to me—such a contrast to the sand and sea of my youth. This would be my home for at least the next three months.

A SCHOOL FOR WARRIORS

Anyone who has been inducted into the military of any nation can tell boot camp stories, so I won't talk at great length about mine. Suffice it to say that Fatah did not go easy on us. Many of our hard-line instructors came from North Korea, North Vietnam, or China—countries that applauded Arafat as a fellow "adversary of imperialism." The instructors didn't speak Arabic, but they certainly got their points across, thanks in part to translators.

I learned to pay attention the very first day when I glanced up at a large sign: "Instructors Are Allowed to Kill 25 Percent of Recruits!" All of us looked at one another, then back at the sign, and took a deep breath. We were from many different places—Qatar, Saudi Arabia, Abu Dhabi, Kuwait (even a Kuwaiti prince was there)—but obviously we would all be marching to one set of orders from this moment on.

I can still hear in my mind the very first instructor barking, "You will follow my instructions in detail! Don't try to do your own thing!" Just then he punctuated his remarks with a volley of live bullets from his Kalashnikov rifle, digging up clumps of earth at our feet. *This little man is serious, isn't he?* I thought.

During certain drills, he would make us run across a field or through heavy brush until he yelled, "Jump!" He would empty an entire clip of bullets in the direction of where our ankles had been. At other times, we crawled along the ground with bullets hissing over our heads. For me, the somewhat spoiled teenager who only a few weeks before had been totally dependent on my mother and the maid to cook for me and do my laundry, it was a quick wake-up call.

> I glanced up at a large sign: "Instructors Are Allowed to Kill 25 Percent of Recruits!"

Our training also included a good deal of judo and karate. Since we were a guerrilla force, we learned how to jump out of second- and third-floor windows while loaded down with gear. We leaped out of jeeps moving at sixty kilometers—over thirty-five miles—per hour. We did high-ropes courses, again in full "battle rattle."

We also had classroom instruction, during which I quickly learned that Fatah had multiple enemies—not just Israel. Most of the Middle Eastern governments weren't happy about having a separate, independent force such as ours operating in their region. They knew the average person was, if anything, more favorable to us than to them, since their military failures were well known. To the average Palestinian hoping for a return to his land, Fatah was more likely to deliver than the government armies. So countries such as Egypt, Jordan, Libya, and even Algeria tried to infiltrate us constantly. They wanted to know what we were up to—and we didn't feel like sharing with them.

The most exciting part of my training was the day I got my very own AK-47 assault rifle, after weeks of practicing with a wooden dummy. It was love at first sight. I sat there on the ground stroking the barrel, the stock, the mechanism. I turned that marvelous weapon from side to side. . . . Truly, a wave of passion rolled over my soul in that moment. What a feeling!

When I learned how to take the weapon apart, it was a flight into ecstasy for me. I spread out a large cloth on the ground, then carefully laid out each piece in orderly arrangement, gazing at it lovingly. "How beautiful!" I whispered to myself. A pleasant shiver ran down my spine. It was mine, all mine.

It was love at first sight.

I cleaned every piece, even though the weapon was already clean. I rubbed the parts down with the soft cloth the weapons expert had provided, until they gleamed in the sun. I held them one at a time to my cheek, like a cat lover would hold up a kitten. Then I applied new lubrication to all the necessary parts before reassembling. What a gorgeous creation it became once again in my hands!

I assembled and disassembled this rifle numerous times, until I became one of the fastest in my unit. As time passed, I could do it even with my eyes closed. I knew every part instantly by its form. The weapon became almost a part of me, like the fingers of my hand, moving smoothly and instantly at my command.

With this exquisite partner I would pursue the dream of my life:

to destroy Israel. I was totally unconcerned about getting home alive. That didn't matter at all to me. I only cared to press the mission for my people's victory.

UNSEEN THREAT

One day while out on the drill field, I saw an unusual weapon leaning against a tree. It certainly was not an AK-47. It had a telescopic sight and a long, sleek barrel. I stared at it with curiosity.

"You like that?" asked the North Korean instructor through his interpreter.

"It looks really different," I replied.

"Would you like to shoot it?"

"Absolutely!" I picked it up, not quite knowing what to expect. He pointed out a tree branch for me to use as a target.

I took aim. The butt of the rifle rested loosely on my collarbone. I pulled the trigger. The kickback nearly knocked me over, leaving me in intense pain.

"Ha!" the instructor laughed. "Here, let me show you how to do it right. This rifle has a much longer range than that AK-47, so it kicks harder." He showed me how to press the butt tightly into my shoulder.

That was my introduction to the Simonov, which was specifically designed for assassinations from a distance. It had a silencer to reduce the noise of the shot and to limit the muzzle flash. I became eager to master this weapon and learn what it took to be a sniper.

By now I had become a group leader. This meant I got an additional weapon, a handgun. I was also issued a bayonet, which could be attached to the rifle muzzle.

More than in weaponry, however, I needed training on the mental aspects of sniping. They taught me how to sit or lie absolutely still for hours on end. In fact, some of the exercises went on for three or four days, around the clock. They wanted to see how long I could endure the pressure of being totally isolated in a strange locale, with little water or food, waiting for the target to come into view at last.

I was not allowed to change position. I had to become part of the tree, as it were. My hands and face were covered with camouflage. Sometimes I wanted to jump out of my skin. But I tried to discipline my emotions, my thoughts, and my bodily functions to stay hardened and under control.

A sniper's work is cloaked in secrecy. Not even my buddies in Fatah knew what I was doing. They only noticed that sometimes I would be gone for a few days, and then I would return. The instructor said my future assignments would usually come by telephone up to a week in advance. I would call a certain man—I met him only one time—who would give me the target and location. He would also say where I could pick up my Simonov; naturally I wasn't allowed to walk around with one of those all the time. If I did, everyone in Fatah would know what I was up to—including the spies among us.

My first sniper assignment came during the cold season. As I moved silently toward my target, I was nervous—but also joyful. Finally I was going to get to do something to help my people! While the high and mighty of this world kept talking and debating and shuffling papers, I would be *doing* something. I'd be taking action in the real world, on actual ground that rightfully belonged to us.

I crouched on top of a warehouse and began my vigil, waiting for the arrival of a certain person I cannot name. I will only say he had done our cause a lot of harm.

The winter chill crept into my bones. I forced myself to concentrate. Looking through the telescopic sight, I watched village people come and go. The hours dragged on. *Why am I doing this? Why should I erase this life?* I asked. I then reminded myself of the answer: *This is helping the Palestinian people. This is removing one of their proven enemies.*

Eventually, after some four hours, the target came walking into view. I studied his face in the crosshairs of my scope. I made sure his features matched the description I had been given. I saw the way his nose flared slightly.

I concentrated on staying calm. I literally forced myself to stop breathing. I pulled my finger back ever so slowly toward the trigger point. I closed my eyes so I wouldn't see, or react to, the moment of impact. Then softly . . . softly . . . I advanced the trigger another millimeter. The firing pin hit the percussion cap. The charge exploded.

I opened my eyes to make sure my bullet had found its mark. It had! That man would never again cause pain and sorrow to our people. I immediately jumped down to the ground and dashed away unnoticed.

Why am I doing this? Why should I erase this life?

Back in the camp, I realized with surprise how mentally exhausted I was. Killing someone is neither easy nor insignificant. You think right away about what you've done. Especially if you planned the act ahead of time. It's different from being in a hot battle: there, you kill on instinct to avoid getting killed yourself in the next two seconds. But when you've laid an ambush and deliberately set the trap to destroy another human being, it takes its toll.

FINAL EXAM

Not long afterward, my sniper training was put to use in a group operation. My unit had to wade across the Jordan River at a shallow spot and move several kilometers into the West Bank. There we would seek to neutralize a small Israeli base. Our target was strictly military; that was a cardinal rule in those days. No harming of civilians whatsoever.

Around two o'clock in the morning, my troops cautiously and silently laid explosive devices in place around the base. We worked slowly; it was better to be quiet and take longer than to arouse somebody's attention. There was no rustling or foot shuffling to be heard.

Finally, all the bombs were in place and wired. Once again, we looked each other in the eye and took a deep breath. It was now close to three o'clock. We retreated to the nearby thickets and got our weapons ready for action.

Our detonator pushed the button. *Ka-boom!* The explosion was tremendous. Dirt and shrubbery flew everywhere. Even we, who knew what was coming, shuddered under the impact. But we were back in control of ourselves immediately, squinting through our scopes for Israeli soldiers as they came pouring out of their buildings in a terrified state. That was the goal of the exercise.

We fired away, dropping as many soldiers as we could with our well-aimed shots. Empty bullet casings hissed over our ears. Then we swiftly ran for our preplanned exit routes, crossed the river, and disappeared back into Jordanian territory.

Our leaders gave us some time off after this assignment. We were not rushed out to another engagement for at least three weeks. They left us alone—so much that I began to worry if we'd done something wrong. But there would be plenty of action in the not-too-distant future.

Before that, however, came the "final examination" of our training: a survival challenge. Each of us was dropped off in a desolate place somewhere in the bush, with orders to get back to camp within three days. We were given no water—just a few biscuits, which were salty and therefore thirst-producing. We had been trained to know which grasses and fruit were edible. We could identify leaves that contained moisture we could suck out.

We also knew, however, that if we got careless at any time, Israeli soldiers might well be in the area to confront us. In fact, at one point alongside a small river, I heard Hebrew being spoken on the opposite bank. I ducked down and waited, holding my breath. What if they had scouts on *this* side of the river? I huddled, immobilized, until the voices stopped for a long time.

Hunger began to grip me by the second day. I tried to ignore the distraction so I could concentrate on the terrain and the danger signals. But it was hard. Then I smelled something odd. What was it? I followed the smell until I came upon . . . a dead donkey. Flies were buzzing all about. The stench was pungent.

But I was terribly hungry. I couldn't just walk away. I got out my knife and looked for a place on the flank that wasn't too decayed.

I cut off a piece. After all, my name meant "butcher," didn't it? I considered building a small fire and roasting it. That would have been safer for my digestion—but the Israelis might have seen the smoke.

I ate the meat raw that day. (Don't tell my mother.) It gave me enough sustenance to get back to camp, thereby passing my test. And I didn't even get sick.

CHAPTER 5

YOUNG
WARRIOR

OUR SURPRISE VICTORY OVER THE ISRAELIS at al-Karameh that day in March of 1968 had electrified the Arab world. Within forty-eight hours, some five thousand new volunteers had signed up to join Fatah. Even King Hussein of Jordan traveled to the town, dressed in battle fatigues, to have his picture taken beside a burned-out Israeli tank. Smiling for the camera, he swept aside previous caution and declared, "We are all *fedayeen!*"—freedom fighters.

A couple of weeks later, an enormous demonstration filled the streets of the capital city, Amman, to honor the dead. Arafat was at his peak of eloquence that day: "The sons of refugees, who once stood in line before UNRWA* to get a sack of flour, a handful of beans, or a blanket, have now arisen to fill the fighting ranks. It is they who will write the new history of Palestine under the watching eyes of the Arab world."

Even the Israelis knew that something very big had happened. Gideon Rafael, director-general of the Israeli Foreign Ministry at the time, would later write in his memoir, "The operation gave an

---

*United Nations Relief and Works Agency

enormous lift to Yasser Arafat's Fatah organization and irrevocably implanted the Palestinian problem onto the international agenda, no longer as a humanitarian issue of homeless refugees, but as a claim to Palestinian statehood."[1]

The morale among my comrades and me could not have been higher in those days. We were ecstatic at what we had accomplished—even as we went on living in the bush, eating canned food and crusty bread, wearing uniforms that didn't fit, and going weeks without a shower. We told ourselves we weren't sleeping in a five-star hotel but rather in the thousand-star hotel of Mother Nature! We grew ever more confident, aggressive—and cocky.

The more missions we undertook, the more our mental state adjusted to the act of killing. We told each other, "We are freedom fighters. We're a special unit on a worthy mission. No one should call us 'terrorists.' In fact, it's the Jews who are the criminals here; they stole our land. We're the legitimate fighting force."

We eventually got to the point of rationalizing even civilian casualties. How? The thought progression went something like this: "Well, Israel has universal conscription. All their young men and even young women have to serve in the army sooner or later. So in fact, there are no civilians! Today's Jewish civilian is tomorrow's lethal soldier."

> The morale among my comrades and me could not have been higher.

If we saw an Israeli civilian carrying a gun, it made it all the easier to justify deadly force against him. "We were acting in self-defense," we said to ourselves and our superiors. "Abu Ammar" (Arafat) could tell his international audiences whatever he wanted about our respect for innocent life. We did what we felt we needed to do.

AT THE WHEEL AGAIN

One day Arafat came to visit our base. We sat in a circle all together, talking about various things. I noticed that he seemed to keep staring at me.

After the meeting broke up, he pulled me aside. Looking intently into my face, he said, "What's your name?"

"Jazzar, sir," I replied.

"No, what's your real name?" he persisted.

"I'm sorry, sir," I answered. "Our movement's rules say we are not to give away our real names. So I must not tell it to anyone."

"Yes, I know," he said with a smile. "I made that rule! But I can break it if I want. *So what is your name?*"

"Excuse me, sir, but I have to keep the rule. I must go by the name Jazzar, and that is all."

He let the matter drop at that point, although he kept eyeing me. I wondered if he was remembering me from his visits to my parents' home back in Qatar. I fervently hoped not, because I didn't want any connections to be made.

Not long afterward, I received a secret assignment that had nothing to do with sniping. I was told instead that on that day, I would become one of Arafat's chauffeurs! I had no idea how this came about, or how long it would last, but I was glad to take any job that would put me closer to my hero.

Of course, there were precautionary measures to follow. His black Land Rover had bulletproof windows that were darkened, so no one on the street could see who I was driving around. I was told the destination only after he got into the car; he was always very tight-lipped about where he was going next. The biggest rule, however, was this: *No stopping for anything or anybody.* Full throttle ahead in all situations, no matter how crowded the avenue or narrow the alley. I was to lean on the horn and keep moving, even if I had to jump the car onto the sidewalk.

> On that day, I would become one of Arafat's chauffeurs.

Soon we were on our way. Tearing through the streets of Amman, I would sometimes look in my rearview mirror only to see pedestrians shaking their fists at me and cursing. Arafat, on the other hand, always seemed to be pleased when I chauffeured him. "Good job!"

he would say. "The only thing is, your driving is going to give me a heart attack!" After one trip, he added, "When I die someday, it won't be because of bullets, but because you've scared me to death on the road."

I took that as a compliment.

MY OWN LITTLE ARMY

One day, life changed dramatically for me yet again. My commander came to me, saying, "Jazzar, we have a new assignment for you. We want you to train the young people of our camps." These were boys aged nine to thirteen whom Fatah put through a six-month program. They would stay in their parents' tents to eat and sleep, but they would come to my sessions every day. Their assignment: to protect refugee camps from our enemies while the men of the camp were away at war.

I, of course, was still only a teenager myself. That was viewed as an advantage, because I could easily relate to my young charges. I could win their allegiance by playing football (what Americans call "soccer") with them and having wrestling contests and stone-throwing competitions.

I had a great time with these kids. They quickly began looking up to me as their "general." They were my own little army. I taught them mathematics and geography—that is, such facts as how many rounds per second you can fire with an AK-47, and how the map of the Middle East *really* ought to be drawn. I taught them how to listen for subtle signals of an intruder getting close, and how to let the adults know what was happening. "You guys will be our eyes and ears," I said. "In this way you will protect your mothers and sisters."

I even gave them specially prepared cassette players, so that when a stranger would approach the camp entrance after dark, they could push a button, and a deep male voice would boom out, "Anybody there?" or "What's going on out there?" Practicing this was funny at times, when the kids would lip-synch the words and then crack up laughing.

I drilled them in karate and judo, just as I had been trained. I taught them rousing songs to buck up their fighting spirit. Then starting at about age eleven, when they were physically strong enough, they began getting weapons training. Some of them were afraid to touch a machine gun at first, so I would appeal to their pride. "Come on, you are the elite!" I would shout. "We chose you because you're strong. You're courageous and brave. You're going to help free your people. The grown-ups can fight the Jews only because you protect the camps. You cover the back of the mighty Fatah!"

Some boys would rise to the challenge while others would shrink in fear. When the lessons got intense, some of them even wet their pants. I promptly sent them home. I was interested only in the best. These boys would perform an important role now—and when they grew older, they would make great Fatah fighters in the regular ranks.

Naturally, our Jordanian hosts did not appreciate the sight of twelve-year-old Palestinians strutting down the street with assault rifles in their hands. We were ignoring the laws of the nation where we lived. But we didn't worry about that; we knew we had to protect ourselves because nobody else was going to do it. And children were key players in that protection.

When I reflect today on what I did with these boys, I feel very sad. I jerked them out of childhood way too soon. I turned them into little monsters. They couldn't be sensitive or playful; I insisted they be tough and ruthless. I made them willing to die on the spot if necessary. What I did was atrocious.

Today I see kids in the Gaza Strip who will stand in the middle of the street and face down an approaching Humvee or even a tank, showing no fear whatsoever. They don't care for their lives or anyone else's. If asked, they are quite willing to strap on a suicide vest of explosives and head out to cause mayhem. They are old before their time.

But back when I was the seventeen- and eighteen-year-old trainer, I couldn't see any of this. I was entirely blind to the psychological destruction I was causing in a new generation.

RAMBO GUY

After four or five months of this work, I was called back to the front and put in charge of a small unit of men. The day-to-day relationships with our Jordanian hosts seemed to deteriorate as time went by. We brought some of this on ourselves, to be sure. I would go into the city carrying my rifle, a full bandolier of bullets slung across my chest, hand grenades swinging from my belt—a veritable Rambo. After I had drawn sufficient attention on the street, I would swagger into a theater to watch a movie, making everyone nervous around me. It was all part of showing how tough I was.

The Jordanian police were actually afraid of us because their firepower was not as heavy as ours. They never had the courage to interfere with me when I would engage in one of my fun "sidelines," namely harassing followers of Christ. Christians made up less than 3 percent of Jordan's population, so of course they had no clout. If I found out about a house where Christians lived, I would swing by and toss a hand grenade into it—if not a burst of machine-gun fire. Nobody took steps to stop me. Only back in my Fatah circle would I be criticized for this. "It's not necessary," my commanders would say. "Our real enemy is Israel, remember?" I brushed them aside.

> I would go into the city carrying my rifle, a full bandolier of bullets slung across my chest, hand grenades swinging from my belt—a veritable Rambo.

We started hearing rumors that the Jordanians might have arranged some sort of cooperation with Shin Bet, the Israeli secret service. More than once, our operations against Israel seemed to run into stiff resistance. Had someone tipped them off? We started withholding information from the Jordanians for our own protection.

One day I got a tip that the Jordanian crown prince would be traveling through a certain area. I was pretty sure he'd had something to do with our recent troubles. "Okay, men," I said to my group, "today we have an opportunity to greatly help our cause.

Come with me." I had no authorization to do this; I just took matters into my own hands. I positioned my men along the road where I knew the prince was going to come.

I didn't tell them *who* was coming because there could have been a spy in my own group. I only said to be on alert.

Sure enough, along came an impressive government convoy—three Chevrolet Suburbans in front carrying bodyguards and escorts, then three black Mercedes limousines, then two more Suburbans followed by army trucks carrying luggage and supplies. Which limo carried the prince? I couldn't tell.

"Hit the middle car!" I ordered, entirely guessing. We let loose with a rocket-propelled grenade (RPG). Immediately the middle Mercedes went tumbling off the road and down a mountainside as it burst into flames.

The other two limousines sped off in a furious cloud of dust, while the military vehicles stopped to begin rescue efforts. We immediately ran for cover.

A few days later, I learned I had guessed wrong. The crown prince was in one of the other two limos, not the middle one. I had failed to get my man.

But one of my guys, unfortunately, started boasting about our little escapade. The Fatah leaders heard about it and called him in for questioning. The Jordanian government was pressuring them to find out who had engaged in this renegade attack. The Fatah leaders turned him over to the government, who forced him to start naming names.

By that time, however, we had split up and headed for different areas. They never managed to chase us down. The government did hang onto the list, though—a list that would come back to haunt me in the future.

DEBATES AND DISTRACTIONS

As the year 1969 rolled on, my life as a Fatah fighter seemed to grow more complicated. Other Palestinian action groups—the PFLP (Popular Front for the Liberation of Palestine), the DFLP (Democratic

Front for the Liberation of Palestine), and others—began doing things that were stupid, in my view, such as ambushing an Israeli school bus full of children, or hijacking commercial airplanes. This only aroused the ire of the powerful Western nations and undercut Arafat's leadership of the PLO. These groups, if they were desperate, would even come to steal our weapons and ammunition.

There were arguments within our own ranks, too, about whether the future Palestinian state should be Muslim only or should welcome people of other faiths. If we set up an open society, that would win us many friends in the West. But it would also entail letting Jews come along with the Christians, Hindus, and others. Could we really tolerate that? Wouldn't they be dangerous? The debates ran long into the night.

We also noticed some of the senior men around Arafat becoming greedy. The money they raised on their various tours didn't always make it back to the general fund. All these distractions made it harder to concentrate on the central mission of taking back our Palestinian homeland.

But we couldn't afford to let down our guard. The Israelis were increasingly clever. One night very late, I was driving a truck full of supplies back to our camp in the mountains. We were holed up in a series of caves so remote they could be reached only by ladders. It was well past midnight, and as I drove through a heavily wooded area, I started worrying. What if somebody were to attack me on this narrow road? I was carrying not just food but guns and ammunition as well. One well-placed rocket would turn the whole truck into a fireball.

I kept driving. The van had no radio, and I struggled to stay alert. I stopped once or twice to splash water on my face. Then I started singing Fatah fight songs to keep myself awake. Finally I made it to the top of the mountain, from which the supplies would have to be hand-carried down the steep slope to our caves. I slumped down in my seat and went to sleep until daylight came.

The eastern sky began to lighten with the arrival of a new day. I woke up. Getting out of the truck, I climbed down the slope. Suddenly, a heartbreaking sight greeted my eyes. Death and destruction were everywhere. The IDF had bombarded our hideaway while I slept at the top of the ridge. Their barrage had been so precise that the rockets had flown exactly into the caves, exploding inside the mountain. My comrades had no chance.

How had the Israeli strike been so surgical?

Then it dawned on me. Several days before, we had hosted a delegation from Europe and had carelessly given them a tour of our mountain fortification. They seemed so friendly to our cause. . . . But quite possibly their group included an Israeli spy who had left behind an infrared homing device. How else could their rockets have zeroed in on the bull's-eye?

If I had not stopped to rest at the top of the mountain, I would have been present for the massacre. Now I was still alive to fight another day—but my friends were not. I slumped down to ask myself whether we could really win this war over the long haul. Yes, we were scoring a victory every now and then. But were we making headway? Was there another strategy, a different approach, to reach our goal? I wasn't sure.

I still believed wholeheartedly in our cause. As long as we Palestinians were homeless, the Jews should not enjoy peace. We deserved justice for what had been snatched away from us. But the tactics for getting that justice—did we truly have them figured out?

What about all those people I had killed as a sniper? They were hated enemies, yes—but they were also human beings, with families who mourned the loss. Was this really the best way to solve our situation? I did not think often about these questions, but once in a while, they would creep to the surface of my mind.

BLACK SEPTEMBER

By 1970, the Jordanian army was no longer subtle about its efforts to restrict us. They actually attacked a refugee camp close to Amman that June, killing hundreds. Times were harder. The euphoria of al-Karameh had definitely faded by now. Rumors spread that King Hussein was on the payroll of America's CIA.

Of course it didn't help that we blew up radio and television stations we felt were critical of us. We also bombed the offices of politicians we thought were soft toward Israel. We even fired a rocket toward the parliament building in Amman.

The average Jordanian in the street still cheered us on; after all, 50 percent of them were Palestinians themselves. But the country's leadership was another matter. In late August the Jordanian army actually besieged our sections of Amman, setting off a bloody clash. On September 2, the impetuous PFLP tried to assassinate King Hussein—and failed. The king's troops were furious, of course, and struck back hard.

That month became known as "Black September," when Jordan decided it had had enough of Fatah and the entire PLO. They ordered us to get out of the country altogether. We couldn't think about fighting the Israelis now; we had a much more immediate problem to manage.

Then, out of the blue, my personal status hit a huge bump.

On a warm, dusty day, I was told to report to the new PLO headquarters west of the capital, where Arafat and his aides had withdrawn. I was to be part of the security detail while the leaders figured out what to do about the king's demand that we evacuate the country.

I reported to Khalil al-Wazir, Arafat's right-hand man, who went by the name of "Abu Jihad." Standing next to him that morning was Salah Khalaf, also known as "Abu Iyad"—my grandmother's cousin. We had not met over the past three years, however.

I saluted.

Suddenly Abu Iyad shocked me by saying, "What are *you* doing here?" He recognized me!

"I was sent here to help with security," I replied, trying to keep my voice steady.

"Come, come, come, come, come!" he ordered, motioning me toward Arafat's office. I thought I would die.

"Abu Ammar, look who we've got here!" Abu Iyad shouted.

Arafat stood up. I could tell by the look on his face that he now recognized me. He smiled. "I was sure I knew you from some-place," he said. "But you were smart enough to keep it from me! Well, you did a good job."

Within minutes, Abu Iyad was on the phone to my father in faraway Qatar. "Guess what—I have your son Taysir standing right here before me! Would you like to speak with him?"

He extended the receiver to me. I reluctantly took it. "Hello?" I said.

The voice I had last heard nearly three years before telling me not to do anything sudden was smooth and calming. He did not berate me. "It is good to hear you again," he said to me.

He then continued, "Your mother is not well. She worries about you constantly. Sometimes in the night, she gets up and goes out in the street in her nightgown looking for you. So you come home now—only for a few days. She needs to see that you are still alive. Then you can go back to the front."

There was no way I could resist my father's instruction. He was, after all, being more reasonable than I had expected. If my mother truly was distraught, I needed to show respect by coming to her.

"All right, Father," I replied. "I will come."

Fatah arranged for a ticket, and the next day I boarded a flight at Queen Alia International Airport, headed for Doha, Qatar. I wore civilian clothes. Sinking into my assigned seat on that plane, an odd feeling came over me. I carried no weapon—and didn't need one. For the first time in years, I didn't have to stay alert. I could relax.

I gazed out the window as the plane rose up and over the terrain below where I had lived and fought. I wondered if Fatah would still be there when I got back. Then I fell asleep.

We landed two hours later in Doha. I stood in the customs line, reading all the familiar signs. This was where I had lived from age ten to seventeen. Soon I would see my family again.

I approached the agent in the booth and handed him my pass-port, which had been issued by Jordan. He studied it carefully. He looked toward a piece of paper that lay to one side. He then said to me, "You may proceed."

"But what about my passport?" I said, stretching out my hand. "Aren't you going to stamp it and give it back to me?"

He only motioned toward the exit with his hand. He wouldn't answer my question. "You may proceed" was all he would say.

CHAPTER 6

SIDELINED

OUTSIDE THE AIRPORT, an impressive car was waiting to whisk me away to a reception hosted by a prince who was friendly to Palestinians. My service to the cause of justice was honored with speeches and gifts. Soon I was back at my home, receiving the welcome embrace of my parents and other family members.

It was wonderful to see my mother again. She wept with joy to know that I was still alive and well. What a celebration we had together that evening!

But a few days later, when I found out my father had tipped off the customs department to confiscate my passport, I was upset. "Why did you do that?" I asked.

"You need to finish your education, son," he replied.

"You tricked me!" I said, raising my voice. "I've been fighting like a grown man for the honor of our people. And you want me to go back to *high school?*"

He said, "The PLO needs members who are smart. How good are you for the cause if you know little? I only got to go up through the sixth grade. You have an opportunity like few other Palestinians. Get a university degree. Then you can do whatever you like—even work in the Fatah leadership if you want."

We'd already had this conversation—three years before. I found it even more frustrating this time around. I had seen a lot more of the world by now—its problems that cried for answers, the realities of fighting and dying, the magnetism of great leaders committed to action. But what could I do? My father had me in a trap.

"I've been fighting like a grown man for the honor of our people. And you want me to go back to *high school*?"

So back to school I went. Here I was, almost twenty years old, a seasoned sniper who had already survived vicious combat, now walking the hallways with fifteen- and sixteen-year-olds. Hour after hour I sat dutifully at a desk, listening to boring lectures and barely containing my resentment.

The only pleasure for me was entertaining the other students with stories of what I had been doing at the front with Fatah. Everyone wanted to hear what it had been like. As a result, my popularity was great.

But as soon as I got home in the afternoons, I would turn on the television news. There I learned that the Jordanian army was in the midst of annihilating the Palestinian people. Their tank battalions were overrunning our headquarters as well as our refugee camps. Yasser Arafat pled with King Hussein for a truce but got only silence. Meanwhile, Arafat's house was bombed—but he was away at the time. Twice the army encircled him, but he always escaped.

I was so frustrated I could hardly stand it. After one week of fighting, the Fatah losses stood at 3,500 dead and 20,000 apprehended. The newscasters said that whoever could escape was heading north over the mountains into southern Lebanon. Those who were captured by the Jordanians were taken to their secret service headquarters—a torture prison set up in an old palace in the hills outside Amman. Very few came out alive.

Whole camps and bases were burned to the ground. Some were even hit with napalm shells, which I assumed came from the Israelis. The thought of my friends suffering this kind of excruciating pain nearly tore me apart.

Once again I debated with my father. "Why did you pull me out just at this time? I need to be with my men! I wanted to fight until I died—and you prevented that." We both knew that if he had not insisted, I would most likely have been lying in the ashes of a bush camp somewhere, burned or napalmed to death. That thought gave him great relief, of course. For me, it was only a disgrace.

By late September, the Arab League managed to get a ceasefire. By then, of course, most of the damage was already done. Arafat was on the run, and his forces were decimated.

BOILING OVER

This left me a sullen, rebellious young man who saw no purpose in life but to cause problems all around me. I stomped into the Qatari palace one day and went on a rampage of screaming, trying to get the officials there to throw me out of the country. It didn't work. I kept trying to get suspended from school. But my father's connections with the Ministry of Education were too strong for that. They kept putting up with me, even though I didn't deserve their attention.

This is how it went for the next three years. I fussed and fumed my way through life, a permanent cauldron of bitterness and rage. One evening my father said, "Taysir, I have another idea. What if you went to live with your uncle in Abu Dhabi and finished high school there? Would you be open to that?"

I stared at him, pondering the various angles. Moving next door in the Persian Gulf to Abu Dhabi would mean I would have to be supplied with a passport, wouldn't it? Yes! This was a good idea, I agreed. Inside, I was thinking it would put me one step closer to flying back to my comrades.

I went out to the airport a day or two later to see the director of the immigration office. "Look!" I demanded. "I need my passport.

I know you have it somewhere here. Please give it back to me!" For visual effect, I toyed with a grenade in my hand as I spoke, so he would know to take me seriously.

"Calm down, son," the man replied. "We want to help you. But do as your father wishes. We don't want to hurt you. Actually, you are not helping your cause by this kind of demand."

In the end, I walked out empty-handed. This made me far less enthusiastic about going to Abu Dhabi, and in time, my father dropped the subject.

Meanwhile, my patience with school continued to deteriorate. One day my math teacher did something that annoyed me. I jumped up and hit the door with my fist. Then I whipped open my jackknife and lunged at him.

The other students in the room began screaming, while the teacher ran for the other side of the room, where he jumped out a window. Seeing that he had escaped, I turned the knife on myself, opening a cut in my stomach. That was enough for the principal to come and have me taken off to the hospital.

While they were attending to my wound, my older brother and his friend, the chief of police, showed up. He knew me well from past escapades.

When we were alone in the room, the chief asked me, "Why did you do this? Are you crazy?"

"I don't want to be here at all!" I answered.

"All right. Let me see if I can at least help you get out of this situation," he said. "Here is a plan. In just a minute, I want you to start screaming as loudly as you can. Jump up and go smash the window with your fist! You will cut yourself again, but not too badly.

"Then I will go outside and say to the nurses, 'The kid is insane. Lock the door and leave him alone!' After this all calms down, you will be released."

I did as he instructed. For several days they left me by myself. Someone would bring my meal tray, set it down quickly, and dash out the door again. I had lots of time to think. When my injuries healed enough, I was able to leave the hospital.

Of course, that only meant going back to school again. I had accomplished nothing.

By the middle of 1971, the PLO withdrawal from Jordan was complete. The royal troops destroyed the last three bases while three thousand fedayeen fled into the woods. Another eighty were so desperate they convinced themselves they might fare better with the Israelis than the Jordanians. So they headed for the river, where they were promptly captured and imprisoned in Jericho.

Of course, this kind of treatment only spawned more extremism. A new group of guerrilla fighters formed, calling themselves Black September. One of their first acts was to deploy four assassins to cut down the Jordanian prime minister at the entrance of the Sheraton Hotel in Cairo, Egypt, on November 28, 1971. The next May, they hijacked an airplane and demanded the release of Palestinian prisoners. Then in early September 1972, they made their world-famous attack on the Olympic Games in Munich, Germany, killing eleven Israeli wrestlers, weightlifters, and coaches. I could not help but wonder if, given the strange twists of history, I might not have found myself joining this group had I stayed in place with Fatah.

> By the middle of 1971, the PLO withdrawal from Jordan was complete.

Instead, my life was a deadening rhythm of classes and assignments. I hated every day. I could see no future for myself. All the excitement of living was in the past.

THE UNTOUCHABLE

I held a job sometimes, but not for very long. I certainly didn't want to take up my father's trade in the automobile business. I dreamed away my time, causing trouble.

One day in my religion class, I cheated on a test. The teacher wrote the questions on the board, and I copied them down on my paper but included no answers. I wrote down only the questions, widely spaced. Then that evening, I sneaked back into the building, tiptoed into the teachers' lounge, found the test papers, located the teacher's book, and constructed my answers accordingly. I then put my completed test in the stack with all the others.

When the tests were returned to the class a few days later, I was shocked to see my grade: zero. I was incensed.

"Sheik Abdul-Salam!" I shouted. "Why did I get this grade? My answers are perfect! Just look at your own book—you'll see."

The short little man came over to look squarely into my eyes. "Yes, your answers are indeed perfect according to my book. That is because you wrote them *after* the test was given! You cheated—and we don't reward that.

"Maybe you think your family is so well-known and influential that you are untouchable," he continued. "Not so! You're nothing but a bug. I can squash you whenever I like."

I was now absolutely livid. There he stood wearing the silly red hat of a religion teacher, having gained all his wisdom from books . . . and he was reproaching me, the battle-tested warrior who had stood up to Israeli cannons. I had risked my life for things he would never be close to achieving.

"Do you think it makes you Allah to wear that cap?" I snarled. I snatched it off his head as I stood up. "I'll get you!" I warned, then walked out of the classroom.

That evening, I drove through the streets, still fuming. What a little weasel he was. I was nearly shaking with anger. Then suddenly, out of the corner of my eye, I saw a familiar form in a car passing the opposite way. It was my religion teacher!

I screeched into a U-turn and began tailing him. He pulled into a shopping mall and parked. I took the spot right behind him and jumped out, grabbing my revolver as I did. I yelled his name.

He swung around, startled.

Before he could say a word, I shouted, "You think I consider myself 'untouchable,' do you? Well, you're right. That's what I am!"

With that, I fired a shot at point-blank range. He crumpled to the asphalt paving. I jumped back into my car and drove away.

The next morning at school, I was summoned to the principal's office. But then—I could hardly believe my eyes. There waiting for me in a chair sat the religion teacher!

"What?!" I exclaimed in shock. "Didn't I kill you last night?"

"No, thanks be to Allah," he replied. Somehow my bullet had missed him. How could that be?

"Don't worry—I'll get you next time," I said.

That's when the principal spoke up. "So it is true, then? You really shot at my teacher?" I had trapped myself.

I nodded assent to the fact. Soon he called the police to come get me. While we were waiting, he told me, "This is the end of your attendance at this school. You are expelled." I didn't care.

The chief of police, my "friend" after all my earlier escapades, took me away that day. I had committed a serious crime, of course. But once again, my father's connections bailed me out. He began talking with the police, the minister of education, and others in high places. Soon the assault charge against me was dropped.

One government official did say to my father, however, "We need to find a solution for your son. Things cannot go on like this. Please think of something."

FRENCH LESSONS

Not long after this I stumbled across an interesting distraction. I was driving in downtown Doha when I happened to glance at the sidewalk, where a gorgeous young European woman was walking. Her miniskirt captured my attention.

I slowed down and began trailing her to see where she would go. She passed a few blocks and then entered a building marked "European Language Academy." I parked my car and nonchalantly walked inside.

"Excuse me," I said to the man at the reception desk, "but I was just wondering who that person was who entered a minute ago."

He gave me the woman's name and said she taught French at this school.

In a matter of seconds, I found within myself a deep love for learning the French language.

"When does the next term begin?" I asked.

"Next week," came the reply.

"How long is the term?"

"Nine months."

"And what are the costs?"

"Twelve thousand riyals," which would equal around 3,500 US dollars.

That evening at dinner, I launched into an eloquent speech with my father about the importance of my learning French. "I found an excellent academy today!" I said. "I can learn so much there. They teach you really quickly, and it will help me move on in my studies."

My father nodded approvingly. Maybe his unruly son was finally starting to get the message. "That's a very good idea, Taysir," he said. "I would encourage you to sign up, even though it's a little expensive. But we can afford it."

It didn't take long, however, for me to discover that my French teacher was already married to the dean of the faculty. I should have checked that out before enrolling. It did not stop me, however, from flirting with her during class. She was pleasant enough toward me, although she drew the line at my repeated suggestions that we get together outside of class. At the time it seemed all I gained out of this experience was an introduction to the French language—but that was something that would actually serve me well in days to come.

After seven months, I told her I was going to drop the course. "Please don't do that," she requested. "You should at least finish what you've started here."

"No, I don't see the point," I responded. "It has been nice to meet you, anyway." And with that, I was gone.

OUT THE DOOR

My father then sat me down for a talk. "All right, here are your choices," he announced in a firm voice. "England or Egypt—which will it be?" I knew he had connections in both countries, friends who could keep an eye on me.

"No!" I retorted. "I can't stand the British. And the Egyptians are a bunch of cowards. They haven't helped our cause at all. If I have to go somewhere, I want to go to America!" This was not because I liked the Americans any better—after all, they supported the Jews. But I had a boyhood friend already living in the United States, and maybe I could go be with him.

"You are *not* going to that satanic country!" my father announced in a firm voice.

"Why not?!" I shot back. And the argument proceeded from there. Why should he get to run my life at this age? I was old enough to make my own decisions. The only trouble was, I needed his money to carry them out.

I kept resisting him, however, until at the end of 1973, he finally gave in. "Look, you have caused me more problems than all your brothers and sisters combined," he said with a heavy sigh. "I give up. Go wherever you want to go. Do whatever you like. Here is your passport. Tell me how much money you need. Just go, and leave us alone!"

In that moment, when I saw how deep his pain went, my heart felt a bit heavy. Even though he had tricked me into leaving Fatah, even though I had no reason now to go on living or do anything productive, I loved this man. I was sad to hurt him along the way.

> In that moment, when I saw how deep his pain went, my heart felt heavy.

"All right, Father," I said. "I will get out of your way by going to America."

I showed up the next day at the American embassy to seek a visa. The clerk began pulling out documents for me to complete. They wanted to know how much money I had, and how much I would be taking into their country. They wanted to know where I had lived so far in my life. The biggest problem turned out to be their request for a character reference from the country that had issued my current passport: Jordan!

I knew in an instant that I was in trouble. There was no way the

Jordanian government would say I was a good guy. After all, I had tried to assassinate their crown prince.

I went home and told my father about this dilemma. I knew that the Jordanian ambassador to Qatar was a good friend of his. Maybe he could pull some strings.

We went together to see the man in his office. I stood there hoping that maybe his information sources would be incomplete on me. Maybe he didn't know everything I had done while living in Jordan.

"My son needs a reference to travel to America," my father said innocently. "Would you be so kind as to take care of this for us?"

"Of course," said the ambassador. "We would be honored to assist. Anything for a good Palestinian like you."

I tried to keep a straight face. Soon the ambassador said to me, "We'll get the paperwork done, and stop back in a couple of days to pick it up."

"Certainly!" I replied, shaking his hand as we left.

But when I came back, the reference was not yet ready. The clerk explained that this kind of thing had to be cleared in Amman first; they couldn't just do it on their own here in Doha. "But don't worry," he added. "The ambassador will still do it as soon as he receives word from the capital."

A week later, the paper still was not ready. I grew suspicious. The consul said, "The ambassador is busy today, but I believe I can handle the details on this. Have a seat."

"What details do you mean?" I asked as I sat down. "Is there a problem?" I didn't trust this man; everyone knew he worked with Jordanian intelligence.

"Actually, my friend," he said as he shuffled some papers on his desk, "you will need to go to Amman yourself to get the reference. It can't be generated here after all."

I stared at him. This was ridiculous. There was no sense playing games with him. I came out bluntly: "Do you think I'm stupid, or what?"

"What are you talking about?"

"Listen!" I shot back through gritted teeth. "With all due respect, you can take your government and all the Jordanian people and go to he—! I won't set foot in your stupid country again!"

"I beg your pardon?" he said. "Well, this kind of attitude is exactly why they want you to come to Jordan. You have connections to our enemies. Why are you asking for a character reference when you're the devil himself?!"

About this time, the ambassador came out of his office. "What's going on here?" he asked.

"This guy thinks he's Allah," the consul snapped with a wave of his hand. "He just told me the whole Jordanian people could go to he— for all he cared!"

"Did you really say that?" the ambassador said to me, his eyes wide with surprise.

I told the truth. "Yes, I did! And I think you know why. You know what your government has been doing to my people."

"Step into my office, young man," he said calmly.

We eyed one another warily. He showed me to a chair and then declared, "My country hasn't done anything bad to your people. Nothing at all. It's really your people's fault."

I could not argue with that last sentence. So instead I said, "Mr. Ambassador, I'm fed up with this kind of life. I want to leave Qatar. But I am *not* going to go to Jordan. You know exactly what would happen to me there."

"Well, if you're fed up with life, as you say, why not go to Jordan? If you want to die, people there can take care of that for you."

"No, I don't want to give them that satisfaction," I replied. "You know what? Just forget it. I'll find a different way to solve this." With that, I stood up and left.

My next stop was the Qatari chief of police. I didn't need to introduce myself, of course. "I am planning to travel abroad," I said, "and for that I need a certificate of good conduct."

He broke into gales of laughter. "You're hilarious, you know?" he said. "After all you've done around here—and you want such a document? Hardly!"

I began begging him. I told him what had happened with the Jordanian embassy. He kept smiling at the predicament I had created for myself. Finally, he settled down and said, "Well, I'll see what I can do. Come back next week."

When I showed up again, he handed me a signed letter. It was very short. It basically said I had lived in Qatar for such-and-such a period of time. That was it.

I figured I would try this with the Americans and see how far it would get me. I walked into the embassy and gave them my name. They pulled out the file on me that had been started weeks before. I laid out the fee money on the counter. Just then, it dawned on me that I had left the chief of police's letter in the front seat of my car.

But before I could excuse myself to go get it, the clerk said, "How long do you intend to stay in the US?"

Hmm. How should I reply? "I'm not sure," I said at last. "Whatever length you can grant me. How about three weeks?"

That was enough to satisfy her. She located the note that documented my father's financial backing for my trip. "Ah, yes—we know your father's company," she commented. "Okay, come back in ten days. We'll have your visa ready then." She never did remember to ask for the statement of good conduct!

When I returned to the embassy on the appointed day, they handed me my passport with the visa stamped inside. I thanked them and turned away quickly. I flipped the pages—and saw, to my utter amazement, a visa that was good for *five years with multiple entries!* Why in the world had they been so generous with me? What a lucky man I was!

"Father, look what I got today!" I shouted when I arrived home. "I need to fly out of here quickly before the Americans change their minds."

We hustled to buy a ticket, and I began packing. The good-byes with my family were emotional and warm. I didn't know when I would see them again. But everyone knew this was the best option for me, far better than staying in Qatar.

I boarded an Alitalia flight from Doha to Rome on February 12, 1974, just a few days after my twenty-third birthday. The connecting flight, a jumbo jet, took me to Montreal. I then caught a connection to Chicago, and on to St. Louis, then finally a tiny two-propeller plane to Columbia, Missouri, where my friend lived. I might as well have stepped off onto a whole new planet.

CHAPTER 7

STRANGER
IN
A
STRANGE
LAND

FROM THE TINY WINDOW OF THE COMMUTER PLANE, I saw white in every direction as we descended toward the Columbia airport. White sand? If so, I would feel right at home in this place. I searched the horizon looking for skyscrapers. After all, this was the middle of America, correct? Surely its business towers clustered together here in the center of the country.

The minute I stuck my head out the aircraft door and headed down the stairs, I got a rude awakening. The white stuff was not sand but snow—something I had seen only in pictures. The February wind cut through my T-shirt like a bayonet. I fumbled to put on the coat I had bought in the Rome airport, then hurried across the tarmac to get inside the terminal.

"Taysir!" I heard my friend's voice. "You made it! Welcome to America!" What a great feeling it was to see Hassan* again; I'd known him since I was five years old back in Jiddah.

"Wow, it's cold here!" were the first words out of my mouth.

"Yes, it's wintertime, all right," he said. "But wait till summer comes. It gets plenty hot. You'll see."

_____
*Pseudonym

We collected my luggage and then headed into the town in his car. He talked the whole way, explaining everything from traffic signs to what certain buildings were. "You can stay with me in my apartment. It's right by the University of Missouri campus. I'm studying engineering there." He went on to describe some of his classes.

All of a sudden, I was no longer listening. I could not believe what I saw out the car window. A man was jogging along the street with absolutely no clothing on! Not a thread. And it was freezing cold out there.

Before I could say a word, two more runners came along following him, just as naked—a man and a woman! I gasped at the sight. My father's words about America being the land of the great Satan echoed in my brain. *So this was what he meant.*

"What is this?" I finally choked out my question, interrupting Hassan's monologue.

"Oh—that's a new fad that just started up here," he said calmly. "They call themselves 'streakers.' For a long time here in America and even in Europe, there have always been nude beaches. But this is different. They want to shock people, so they go running in the streets or out onto a sports field. Or they'll go into a bar that way. Don't worry—it will be over soon."

Coming from the Middle East, where men and especially women cover themselves from head to toe, no matter how hot it gets, this was a jolt to my senses. I didn't fully catch my breath until we settled into his apartment that evening.

Hassan did his best to make me feel comfortable. But of course he had to continue his studies. On one of the first Saturdays, he went to the library to work. I was tired of being cooped up in the apartment with nothing to do, so I decided to go for a walk, since it had gotten a little warmer outside.

I explored the neighborhood and came across some interesting shops. I had no map, and I didn't know enough English to be able to read the street signs. When I decided to head back toward home, I wasn't sure which way to go. Was my destination down this avenue? Or that one? Gradually, I realized I was lost.

Fear crept over me. How would I ever get back to my friend's place? I chided myself for being afraid. Hadn't I already faced danger in my life? Hadn't I looked into enemy gun barrels with courage? What was the matter with me?

But these were Americans on all sides. They favored the Jews, not me. And I had no weapon to defend myself. If some of them caught me and realized I was lost, they could do terrible things to me. I began to sweat with worry, even though the temperature was still cool.

I kept trying one street after another. The city had now lost its attraction for me. Darkness would come soon. What would be my fate in this scary place? The streets of Columbia, Missouri, somehow seemed more frightening than the underbrush of the West Bank. I wandered on and on, peering around every corner.

Three hours later, Hassan came racing up in his car. "Where have you been?" he shouted out the window. "I've been driving all over looking for you! What were you thinking?"

I crawled into the passenger seat of his car and wept like a little child. I was emotionally exhausted. "Hassan, I have fought in war," I finally said, "and I wasn't afraid of anyone or anything. But today I found out what fear really is."

He laughed and replied, "Well, I'm glad I found you at last. Now you really have to get busy learning English, Taysir. It's the only way you're going to make it here in this country."

NOT SUCH A BAD PLACE AFTER ALL

For the next forty-five days, I didn't leave Hassan's apartment. I immersed myself in two TV programs a day that taught English to children. Hassan brought me the newspaper every day and *Time* magazine every week. I struggled through all of it, trying to grasp as much as I could.

I already knew the English alphabet from my French classes back in Qatar. So I was acquainted with the various sounds. I kept trying to put them together into the English words I heard all around me. Whenever Hassan's friends would come over for a party, I would pick up more of the casual terms and slang.

Soon I found out that the American school system had a marvelous alternative for finishing high school: the GED (General Educational Development). You didn't have to sit through all the classes like I had been struggling to do back home. If you managed to pass five big tests, you could graduate quickly. What a great invention! I immediately set my sights on this goal.

The more time I spent with Americans, the more I realized that they could be nicer than I had expected. No one seemed to want to kill me. No one tried to abduct me. I picked up no hint of a secret army waiting to get me. Instead, people were congenial and open. Their attitude was friendly and cheerful. I was genuinely surprised.

I met a few Arabs who were attending the university, and they spoke positively about their experience in this country. There seemed to be a great value for equality and fairness. Nobody called me "refugee" or "immigrant." I kept waiting for somebody to put down the Palestinians and praise the Israelis, but the subject didn't seem to come up.

Maybe I should stay in this country, I said to myself. *It has a lot of advantages, doesn't it?*

I kept waiting for somebody to put down the Palestinians. But the subject didn't seem to come up.

So I brought up the subject with Hassan and his friends. "I'm thinking of staying here in America," I said. "How would I do that?"

"What kind of visa do you have?" they asked.

"A five-year, multiple-entry one. I can stay for six months, but then I have to leave for six months before I can get back in again."

"Well," they explained, "if you want to become a permanent resident and get a job, you have to get what is called a 'green card.' It's your key to the future."

"How do I get a green card?" I asked.

They started laughing. "Well, you can go through all the application process on your own—or if you want the easiest and quickest route, you simply marry an American woman!"

Hmm. Now there was an idea I would have never thought of by myself.

ON THE HUNT

That spring, Hassan decided to work in Kansas City for the summer, 125 miles west. I went along, of course. By now I had completed my GED and was ready to take classes in business management.

We talked a lot about how to meet eligible girls. "Go dancing in a nightclub," somebody said. "It's a good place to get started."

I frankly admitted to Hassan that I wasn't interested in tying the knot for life here. "That's all right," he said. "You can always get a divorce after a year or so, once you get your green card. It's not a problem." I nodded my head in agreement. This would be the plan.

One Thursday night, he and I went to a club. As we sat down at a table and began surveying the crowd, my eyes landed on an attractive young blonde with big blue eyes who sat laughing and drinking with some friends. "How about her?" I said to Hassan, nodding in the girl's direction.

"Okay," he said. "Here's what you do first," he began, proceeding to give me instructions.

I promptly stood up and walked toward her. "Hello!" I said, putting on my best smile. "Could I interest you in a dance?"

Her eyes turned cold. She hesitated as she looked at me. Then she shook her head no and returned to her friends.

I walked away a little crestfallen. *Now what?*

When I told Hassan what had happened, he wasn't discouraged. "That's all right. Give her some time. Try again later on."

A half hour later I wandered back in the blonde's direction again. "Are you sure you wouldn't like to dance?" I asked.

Again, she looked at me with a cool stare. "No, not really," she replied.

What was her problem? She must be blind or something. I went back to my table once again. "She turned me down again!" I reported.

Hassan started laughing. "Well, how about that! I bet you're never going to get her," he said.

He was challenging me. "Oh, really?" I replied. "All right—put your money on the table! I'll take that bet." He smiled and pulled a five-dollar bill out of his wallet. I thought, *How cheap can he be?*

I took a deep breath, then stood up and returned to the girl for the third time. Putting on my most pitiful accent, I said, "Me like sis music, but—you pleez dance wit me?"

She smiled for the first time. Then she extended her hand, and we moved onto the dance floor together. I held her waist as we began moving to a Jim Croce tune, "I'll Have to Say I Love You in a Song."

We had a nice time, but the place was getting warm, so we found a door to the fire escape in the back of the club. As we moved toward the door, I caught Hassan's eye and winked. He nodded. We began talking in the cool night air. I found out her name was Karen. I explained how to pronounce my name: tay-SEAR.

"Where are you from?" she asked.

"Palestine," I answered. "But my family lives in Qatar for now. That's out in the Persian Gulf."

"I see," she replied with a bit more coolness.

She then changed the subject. "How come you wear your hair so long in the back?" she asked. It was long and curly, down almost to my shoulders. She wasn't being critical, she just wanted to know.

"Why, don't you like it?" I replied.

"Well, ummm . . ."

"I see a lot of guys at the university who wear their hair this way," I said.

She responded, "You'd look better if you made an exception."

I wasn't used to young women being this forward in their comments. But I wouldn't be upset. After all, I had a mission to accomplish with this girl.

We kept talking for a long time, and the conversation seemed to run smoothly. *This was a nice girl,* I told myself. I wondered what she thought of me, apart from my background (and my hair). There was a lot I would never tell her, of course. But for the moment, I tried to come off as likable and safe.

In the end, I said, "Can I get your telephone number?"

"No, I had a nice time, but I don't think so," she replied.

"I would really like to get to know you," I said. "We have a lot in common."

"Well, I guess we could talk," she said, and finally gave the number I wanted. I wrote it down on a strip of paper from my pocket.

I called her the next day, Friday, and asked her to go out with me that night. She again said no, and I asked why. She told me she already had a date that night with another guy.

"Okay, then how about Saturday night?" I persisted.

"You know, I think it would be best if we just remained friends for now and talked on the phone. That's enough."

I didn't have a comeback for that answer, so we said good-bye. I felt she resented me for some reason. I wanted to know why.

The next day, Saturday, I walked to the phone booth on the street below our apartment to call again. It was cloudy, and as we talked, it began to rain. She was surprised that I called and still seemed distant to my questions.

Finally, I decided to get to the bottom of this. "Karen, I feel like you're a little cool toward me. I really want to know—what is wrong? Is it that you're dating this other guy?"

She paused. "Well, actually, my 'date' last night was not with another man," she confessed at last. "It was with my son. He's six weeks old."

"Really!" I exclaimed. This was certainly a new piece of information.

She then went on to tell me about her relationship with a Persian guy, a sergeant in the Royal Iranian Air Force, who had been stationed the year before at Forbes Air Force Base out by Topeka, Kansas, for training. She shared about that situation and Benali, the boy who had been born.

> She resented me for some reason. I wanted to know why.

The sergeant, however, had returned to his home country, leaving Karen to fend for herself with a new baby.

I felt so badly for her—especially since she had been abandoned by someone from my part of the world. I thought maybe I could repair some of the damage if I married her, got my green card, and helped her raise her son, at least for the time we would be married. So I kept pushing for a relationship. In fact, I stepped out that day and did a very Middle Eastern thing: I asked her right there on the phone to marry me. Naturally, she was shocked by the abrupt proposal and said, "Oh, my goodness, I hardly know you!"

I insisted that I wanted to meet her family. We kept talking. Finally she said, "Where are you calling from?"

"I'm in a phone booth on the street," I answered. "That sound you hear is the rain pouring down."

"We've been talking for four hours, and you've been out in the rain all this time?!" she exclaimed.

"Yes!"

She was impressed, to say the least. She asked me to come join her family for dinner on Monday, which would be Memorial Day. *Okay, I'm making progress!* I said to myself.

"The only thing is," I added, "I don't have a car. Is there any chance you could pick me up?" She said she would.

We hung up at last. I headed straight for a barber shop.

GETTING TO KNOW YOU

When Karen arrived Monday afternoon, she noticed right away. Coming in the door, she commented, "Nice hair!" as she reached up to touch the back of my head.

That was the first real date of many for us. We talked about lots of things with ease. We found out that we both liked Datsun cars and dancing. We talked about her schooling hopes as well as her job at a bank. I got to meet her son, who was a beautiful baby with big blue eyes.

I found out she and her family were Catholic. She had four sisters and one brother. Her father, a short Irishman with a big personality who had his own architectural firm, was named Larry. Her mother, Mary Lee, was a kind and very welcoming woman.

Whenever Karen and I talked about the Middle East, I kept things short and simple. I did tell her a little about my involvement with Fatah, that I'd been part of a group to "try and help the Palestinian people." That was about the extent of the explanation.

I was more interested in edging back to the subject of marriage, which I managed to achieve by summer's end. She, being in a vulnerable spot now with a baby to support, was open to the idea. And, of course, this had been my goal from the beginning. I felt I was really making progress. In my first few months in this new country, I had learned its language and gotten my GED—and now I was on my way to a green card.

We talked about whether her parents would go along with our plans.

"They're pretty skeptical about Arabs," she admitted. I did my best to change their assumptions. For one dinner at their house, I showed up with *two* dozen roses—one bouquet for Karen, the other for her mother.

Her father, Karen told me, hung out most afternoons in a neighborhood bar called Medlin's. I went there one afternoon and scouted out the place, asking the bartender about Larry Whelan's favorite brand of whiskey. I made sure they had it available.

> In my first few months in this new country, I had learned its language and gotten my GED—and now I was on my way to a green card.

The following week I invited Larry for a drink and suggested we meet at Medlin's. When we finally got down to the real question, his conclusion was, "I don't really want to stand in anybody's way. She's twenty-one, which is old enough that she can decide for herself."

On another occasion, Karen and I turned to the subject of religion.

"You wouldn't expect me to turn Muslim, would you?" she wanted to know.

"No, of course not," I assured her. "You're fine just the way you are."

Neither one of us was all that devout, to be honest. I wasn't going to a mosque here in America, and her attendance at Mass was spotty as well. Nevertheless, she explained, "I have always wanted to be married in my church. We'll need to go see my priest. He's been a friend of my family for a long time."

"Okay," I said.

The appointment did not go well. We sat down in his office, and after a few pleasantries, Karen introduced me and said we wanted to arrange a wedding.

The priest looked at me. Then he blurted out, "Karen, are you sure he's not just marrying you to get a green card?"

I lurched back in my chair. Karen stiffened as well. I could tell she was offended. She swallowed once before composing herself. "Father John," she said at last, "I know Taysir very well. He has asked to marry me because of *me*—not for some legal benefit. We love each other, and we want to be husband and wife. Trust me, please."

"Well, he would need to go through the classes for marriage in the church," the priest responded, changing the subject. "Those are the rules, as I'm sure you are aware, Karen."

"How long is the course?" I asked.

"Nine months."

There was silence for a moment. Then Karen said, "Well, we can't wait that long. His visa requires that he leave in another month. Isn't there another way?"

The priest leaned back in his chair. "I suppose you could have a civil wedding, and then later, after the classes have been completed, you could come back to me." We could tell he wasn't happy about this option, however.

We excused ourselves and went outside to talk. We then went to her house and aired what we had heard. We spoke with her parents about the faster route. I thought they would be pleased at not having to pay for the full festivities. But I was wrong. Larry especially had been dreaming of a big wedding for his daughter.

"That would take too much time and planning," I protested. We kept batting around the variables. Finally, in the end, they gave in, allowing us to set our own timetable.

"I DO." (I DO?)

So on October 4, 1974, we stood up in front of a justice of the peace in the Jackson County Courthouse in Kansas City and were married. The ceremony took all of fifteen minutes. We paid the fee, and I even gave the justice a ten-dollar tip.

Karen's parents were there, of course. They hosted a small party afterward, wishing us well. We had no time for a honeymoon; Karen had to be back at work Monday morning. We spent the weekend moving her and young Ben into my studio apartment on Washington Street. There we would begin our marriage.

As far as Karen was concerned, this was a binding commitment for life. She had said, "I do," and that settled it permanently. I said what she wanted to hear that would affirm this understanding on my part as well. She looked forward to growing old with me at her side. In my mind, I was willing to play the role temporarily—at least until the green card was safely in my hands.

Only now did I send a letter to my family back in Qatar explaining what I had done. I figured it was better not to let them know ahead of time. I thought there might be a backlash against having this "infidel woman" from the land of the great Satan as a family member.

The reaction was stronger than I ever imagined. My parents were incredibly angry. They reminded me that I had been promised to the daughter of an uncle there in the Middle East back when she was born. Now I had damaged the reputation of both clans. People would be questioning this girl's reputation, wondering what was wrong with her that I had spurned her as a wife. Nobody else would be willing to marry her.

"I wanted you to become an engineer in America," my father said. "Even when you said you were studying business management and international marketing instead, I was willing to go along with that. Now I find out that you have been spending your time courting women—and have gone ahead and married without any consultation with us!

> She looked forward to growing old with me at her side. I was willing to play the role temporarily.

"That is the end, Taysir. *No more money from the family.* I'm finished with paying your expenses. From now on, you take care of yourself! In fact, I have even cut you out of my will."

Karen and I looked at each other in shock. We really had not counted on this turn of events. I didn't have my green card yet in order to get a job—and my source of income had been abruptly cut off. What were we going to do?

If I dumped this young woman and her baby to run back to my home in Qatar, I would just be repeating the dirty trick they had already suffered once before. They trusted me. They were innocently looking to me to provide for them. I couldn't just disappear.

I had gotten myself into—how did the Americans say it?—a real jam.

CHAPTER 8

PUTTING DOWN ROOTS

I EXPLAINED OUR PLIGHT TO HASSAN and all our other friends, who sympathized with us. "What do I do now?" I asked. "We're going to starve."

"Well, I work in this classy French restaurant down on Forty-eighth and Pennsylvania," said one fellow, "and our dishwasher guy is going to quit. Maybe you could take his place. The food business doesn't seem to be so strict about all the rules when it comes to hiring."

I had never washed dishes even at home growing up, let alone when I was with Fatah. But I was desperate now. And the word *French* caught my ear. It wouldn't hurt to try.

So the next day, I put on my best suit and went to La Méditerranée. It was dark and rustic, with a feel more like a country French place than a bistro. The tables were not yet set up for dinner when I walked in around twelve-thirty. The woman who owned the place with her husband mistook me for a customer.

"*Oui, monsieur,* 'ow can I 'elp you?" she asked in a thick French accent.

"*Mais non, madame,*" I replied. "I'm here to help *you!*"

She stared at me in disbelief: "You 'elp *me*?"

"Yes. A friend of mine told me that you were looking for a dish-washer. I would like the job."

She eyed me from head to toe. "Dishwasher? *Mon Dieu, entrez, come ahead.*" She then called for her husband to come out of the kitchen. She told him that this well-dressed young man had come to do the dishes.

I had never washed dishes even at home growing up, let alone when I was with Fatah. But I was desperate.

Even I laughed at the thought.

"*Mais* so, you speak French?" she asked again.

"*Oui, madame, je parle un tout petit peu.*" (Yes, ma'am, I speak a little bit.)

Soon the husband led me downstairs to pick out a uniform. I changed clothes and then reported back to the kitchen. He began showing me how to run the big dishwashing machine, how to clean the oversized pots by hand, how to mop the floor. Normally, they had two people for this job, he explained, but the other fellow hadn't shown up today. So I would be working by myself.

"I'm sure I will make some mistakes, monsieur," I said.

"That's all right," he replied kindly. "Have you ever done this kind of work?"

"No, not really. But my family has gone to French restaurants, and I always liked them," I said, which wasn't much of a qualification. He said nothing in response.

At six o'clock, the restaurant opened for business. I was soon busy with dirty dishes coming out of the dining room. I did the best I could. I hoped the owner would be pleased.

Around nine o'clock, he said, in his wonderful accent, "Gee, you 'ave never done sis? You arre good! Do you want to stay 'erre with us?"

"*Oui, monsieur*—I would like that very much!" I said enthusiastically.

I soon found out that the job paid only $4.50 per hour, which wouldn't go far. I would need to get a second job for the mornings. I eventually found one as a clerk in a gas station.

But in the meantime, I was closely watching the owner as he cooked. I studied with interest as he created wonderful recipes.

"Do you want to know 'ow to cook, too, *oui*?" he asked me.

"Oh, very much," I replied.

"All rright, come early tomorrrow—I will begin teaching you. But I won't pay you extra."

That was acceptable to me. I started learning the art of French sauces first. Then he showed me how to use the grill. He complimented my speed in learning, and so did his wife. Maybe I wouldn't be washing dishes forever in this place.

TWO VISITORS

Meanwhile, I filled out the government application for permanent-resident status, now that I was married to an American. I paused when I came to the question that read, "Have you ever belonged to a political or military organization? If so, describe."

Should I tell the truth?

I decided it would do no good to lie. The American government no doubt had ways of finding me out. So I put down, *Yes. Fatah.*

Hardly three days later, there was a knock on our apartment door. Two FBI agents stood there, showing their badges. "Mr. Saada?" one of them said. "We'd like to speak with you if we may."

I didn't like the feeling of this.

But I invited them in, and we talked briefly. They asked some factual questions. My English was not the smoothest, of course. So they said, "How about if we come back with someone who can speak Arabic? That would make you more comfortable, wouldn't it?"

"Yes, that would be better," I said. "I have nothing to hide. I'll be glad to answer all your questions. But next time, could you please not be so obvious when you arrive, with your badges and everything? The neighbors will think I'm a criminal."

They agreed.

A few days later they returned with another agent who had studied Arabic with the FBI. It was funny to listen to him. His grammar was correct, but his accent and choice of words were comical.

He set out a small tape recorder on the table between us. I looked at it suspiciously. Then I said, "Wait a minute, please. I'll be right back." I went into the other room and returned with my own recorder, a big machine that was very old, with separate speakers.

"What are you doing?" they asked me.

"Well, I know some of the games that investigators play," I answered. "I just want to make sure that we all have the same copy."

"Okay," they said, laughing. "That's fine with us."

Then the questioning began. One of their queries was, "Are you planning to work for Fatah here in the United States?"

Again, I chose to tell the truth. "If Fatah asked me to do something, like raise money or whatever, I'd be ready in a second. But I wouldn't do anything to harm this country."

"What is the background of that attitude?" they wanted to know. "How have you come to feel this way?"

"Americans have been very nice to me. They have welcomed me with open arms. Nobody has called me a nasty name. I feel the love of the people here, and I want to respect that."

They seemed to believe that I was speaking from my heart.

Then the agent said, "If at some point we needed some information and we were to call on you, would you be willing to help us?"

"If I knew about someone planning to attack this country," I replied, "I wouldn't even wait for your call. I would come on my own and tell you about it."

"What do you think about Fatah and the resistance?" they asked.

"I will tell you the honest truth: I believe it is right to fight against Israel for what they took from my people. Fatah is opposed to violence and terror against civilians. But when it comes to the Israeli military, it's a different story, in my view. I hope you understand my feelings as a Palestinian." I wasn't giving away any secrets here; they already knew I had participated as a Fatah fighter.

We parted on friendly terms that day. Karen, naturally, was very relieved when it was over. And so was I. Once or twice thereafter they called me back to ask a question or get a perspective when something happened in the news. I understood that they were doing their job to protect this country, and I willingly helped them. I appreciated that the FBI played fairly with me in return.

OUT FROM THE SHADOWS

Back at the French restaurant, I kept getting compliments from the owner couple. One evening, the wife said to me, "Taysir, would you like to learn 'ow to wait on people?"

"Oh, yes!" I replied.

She began training me in the art of being a good busboy. Then came the time for me to start. I put on the white tuxedo shirt, the black bow tie, and the black vest. When I entered the dining room with its dimmed lights, it felt like another world from where I had been in the kitchen. It was elegant—but it was also a bit unsettling for me. I suddenly realized that anyone and everyone would be able to see me here.

What if someone from Qatar comes in? I worried to myself. They could possibly know my family. And here they would see me working as a waiter! I would be so ashamed, and so would my parents back home.

That first evening, I still had not calmed down as the customers came and were seated. I tried to remember how to do everything right. At one of my tables sat a middle-aged businessman in an expensive suit with a beautiful young woman. They were deeply engaged in conversation for a long time.

When it was time to clear away their used dishes, I reviewed in my mind how to proceed. I didn't want to mess up anything this first time. The man looked up at me as I worked, smiled, and said, "Thank you, young man." Then he went back to talking to his dinner guest.

I couldn't believe it. This wealthy man had stopped what he was doing to thank me for clearing his table? That would never have happened in the Middle East. There the service personnel get ignored or even insulted.

"You're welcome, sir," I replied with a smile. I decided right then that this gentleman would get my best attention.

I said to the owner later on, "Do you know the man in the dark suit over there with the young woman?"

"Oh, yes," said my boss. "That's Charlie Sharpe. He comes here often. He's president of a life insurance company." I made a note to remember that name.

Thereafter, I always greeted him warmly when he came to La Méditerranée. I made sure he got excellent service. If he happened not to sit in my section, I told his waiter to keep an extra eye on him, because "he's a good man."

I think he could tell I was attuned to his business. He began asking for me when he called in his reservations. We talked often at his table and, over time, became good friends.

> This wealthy man had stopped what he was doing to thank me for clearing his table?

The more contacts I made with our customers, the more I realized that it was hard for them to pronounce my name. "Taysir" just didn't come naturally for them. So I made up a nickname. Starting with the first letters of *Taysir A. Saada,* I came up with *Tass,* making it rhyme with *mass* or *lass.* That proved to be a lot more convenient for everyone.

SURPRISE

After several months, my green card arrived. I held it in my hands and breathed a sigh of relief. I was now welcome to stay in America as long as I wished, as far as the government was concerned. Of course, deep inside I had other plans for my life.

I did not act on my plans right away, however. For one thing, I was falling in love with Ben. What a sweet little guy he was! But by the beginning of 1977, I was finally ready to make my move. Karen would be able to manage life from here on without me, wouldn't she? I tried to convince myself that this was true.

Then, out of the blue came those three little words that get every husband's immediate attention:

"Honey—I'm pregnant."

We had definitely not planned on this! At least *I* had not. This did not fit at all with what I was about to do. But how could I walk away now?

"Oh! That certainly complicates things," I said to her.

"Why? Aren't you happy, Tass? We're going to have a little baby!" She looked a little hurt at my lack of enthusiasm.

I thought up some excuse to cover for what I was actually thinking. But I doubt she was fooled.

On September 13, 1977, our little daughter was born. We named her Farah, which in Arabic means "joy." Karen was certainly pleased, and our son, Ben, then three and a half, was excited to have a sister. As for me, I tried to play the role of proud father. The truth is, however, that on the inside I was conflicted. To a Muslim, the thought of raising a girl in the loose American culture was downright scary.

My feelings about this new responsibility—and other matters as well—would occasionally boil over when I was home. Karen found me to be an angry young husband, even explosive at times. I could be nice and generous in public, of course. I was a charming waiter at work. But the real me, down underneath, was haunted.

My reactions were sometimes beyond the scope of normal behavior. "Tass, please don't be upset with us," Karen would sometimes plead when the children were noisy, or some other event got me agitated. "We can get through this without a fit."

I brushed aside her advice. She didn't really understand the forces that had shaped me into who I was.

I poured myself into my work, putting in longer and longer hours. When the owners of La Méditerranée got ready to sell it, I pushed hard to be the buyer. They said, "Tass, you are a good *capitaine* over the other waiters, a fine employee, but you're not ready to be a proprietor. You need more time in this business." And besides, they already had friends to whom they wanted to sell the place. The man was French, and his wife was German. "Work with them, Tass, and when *they* want to sell, you will be ready."

This disappointed me, but I went along with what they said. The new owners, however, proved to be difficult. For one thing, they continuously fought with each other. The whole restaurant staff was on edge as a result. I began doing things my own independent way, since I knew the clientele better than they did. That resulted in conflict, and they brought in their own manager, demoting me back to a waiter position.

I got mad and quit. But soon their manager gave up, and so the couple asked me to return. I went back more determined than ever to buy the restaurant.

For years they tantalized me with the idea that they might sell to me, but they always changed their minds. I realized they were just stringing me along.

FAMILY CONTACT

When my father came to visit us in 1979, he was impressed with how far I had gotten in this new land. It was his first time to hear my nickname, *Tass*. He liked it. People on the street, or business customers in the restaurant, would cheerfully greet me in their friendly Midwestern way. "Hey, Tass, how are ya? Good to see ya!" My father found that to be unique.

He took note of the comfortable life we had built in just five years. We lived in a nice duplex in a good suburban school district. We had two cars. "How does this all work?" he quizzed me. "Are you selling drugs on the side?"

I laughed heartily. "No, Dad. It's just that I work hard, and this is a land of great opportunity."

Two years later, in 1981, he came back for a second visit. We were even better off by then. He was visibly moved. "My son, I'm proud of you," he said with all sincerity one day. "You've done it on your own. You've made a success of yourself, even without my help."

This statement meant the world to me—especially after he had disowned me following my marriage. I had legitimized myself in his eyes. I felt proud of having earned his approval.

Late the next year, my mother called. She said she was very ill. It pained her to think she might die and not see me again. Was there any way I could come back home for a while? Karen and I began talking about this situation, and in 1983, we packed up the family and made the long move to Qatar. There I opened an import-export business with an old friend of mine, a prince. He had good contacts, and the business prospered. We were doing well financially.

My mother's health rallied. She was elated to meet her grandchildren, of course. And the rest of the family gave us a warm welcome. But it was hard for Karen to come under the limitations of being a woman in a strict Muslim culture. Plus, she didn't know the language. Neither did my children. Ben was nine years old by now, and Farah was six. Unfortunately, for the most part, they stayed indoors and watched a lot of television. They didn't have the means to cross the gap into Qatari society.

> I had legitimized myself in his eyes. I felt proud of having earned his approval.

I had to admit that something was missing for me as well. Although I fully understood this place and how it operated, I chafed under its constraints. The freedom to speak your mind openly was not to be found there. You could get in trouble for your candor much more quickly than in America. In fact, businesspeople began coming to my father after a while to comment about my brash attitude. They found me to be cocky, they said. While they didn't have the nerve to confront me directly, they got their point across by detouring to my father.

After nine months, my mother asked to see me one day. "My son, I thank you for coming back here," she said. "It was a wonderful thing for you to do. I perceive that you truly do love me.

"But," she continued, "I can tell that you are not entirely happy. It's hard for your wife and children, too. If you want to go back to your country, I give you my blessing. You can feel free to go home."

Tears welled up in my eyes as I thought about what she said. Here we were in Qatar, and yet she had spoken to me about "*your* country." Even she could see that this was no longer my home. She had observed my family at close range and had seen that I cared about them. The whole experiment in Qatar wasn't really working, was it?

"Thank you, Mother," I said. "Yes, I really want to go back to America."

Soon after, we returned to Kansas City. I had put down more roots in that place than I'd realized.

CHAPTER 9

A
SLOW
UNRAVELING

WE BOUGHT A NEW HOUSE IN RAYTOWN, MISSOURI, a suburb of Kansas City, and I quickly found a job in a restaurant owned by an Iraqi. The place had potential, but the owner had a drinking problem, and on top of that, he wasn't entirely honest.

So it was a good thing that the owners of La Méditerranée called to see if I would come back to them. Apparently, the business had not fared so well in my absence. "Would you be willing to work for us again?" they asked.

I didn't tell them that in the back of my mind, I had been thinking of trying to open a high-end French restaurant of my own that would eventually drive them out of business. Instead I opted to take their offer. Maybe now that they saw my value, they'd be more open to selling La Méditerranée to me, as I had always wanted.

Sure enough, the business prospered. Sometimes when my old friend Charlie Sharpe would drop by for a meal, I would sit down for a minute beside his table. "Help me figure out how to buy this place," I would quietly murmur. "I really want to find a way to make that happen."

He would give me some pointers on how to proceed. I would try what Charlie suggested, and the owners' response would appear hopeful. But then they would change their minds again. It became like watching somebody pull petals off a flower: "We're willing to sell." "No, we don't think we'll sell now." "Yes, we're open to selling." "Well, we think we want to keep the restaurant after all."

This dragged on all throughout 1986 and 1987. Finally, I ran out of patience.

The manager of Kansas City's big Westin Crown Center hotel was another customer of ours, and he talked to me frequently about the restaurant business. He invited me to come check out his operation. His eighteen-story facility, with 729 rooms, was part of the Hallmark complex and had a very attractive place called "The Brasserie," but the service was terrible. He wanted to know if I would come whip it into shape.

"I know how to manage a fine-dining restaurant that's open in the evenings only," I said. "But three meals a day? That's not my expertise. I would enjoy working here, however. . . ."

"Well, if you want to take a chance, Tass, I'll work with you," he said with a smile.

Now the negotiation was on. "My price is high," I countered. "You won't be able to afford me."

"How much do you need?" he asked.

This was early 1988. "Forty thousand a year, plus benefits," I declared. Now I would learn if he was truly interested in my services or not.

He leaned back in his chair, formed his mouth into an *O*, and blew out a long breath. "That's a lot of money for a restaurant manager," he said.

"I can appreciate that," I replied. "But for me, this is more than a job. I go into this kind of thing totally committed. You've seen what I can do at La Méditerranée. Why don't you go ahead and give me what I said? You'll recover the investment from the way the business takes off, I'm sure."

A day or two later, he phoned to say okay. "Never before in our history have we paid a restaurant manager this much," he added. "But I believe you can make this place a success."

"Very well!" I said. "And in light of that, I need to mention one other thing."

"What is that?"

"I need to bring along my own chef."

"Oh, come on!" he said. "You can't be serious."

"Yes, I am. I know this man—he's French—and he will make all the difference in the food we serve. That's how you get people talking about a restaurant. That's what gets the momentum rolling."

"How much salary will he cost?" the hotel manager then asked.

"Same as me. His contribution to the restaurant is every bit as important as mine."

"There's no way Westin would let me pay a chef that much," he replied. "My boss would have my head."

"Just try it."

To his great surprise, the Westin boss went along with my requirement. Soon came the day in April that I showed up at four in the morning to tackle my first day on the job at The Brasserie.

I'd never overseen a breakfast buffet before, but in the last weeks I'd done some reading to prepare myself, and somehow we made it happen. Lunchtime came off all right that day as well. Then we got to the evening meal, where I was back on familiar ground.

I made changes, of course, as the first weeks and months unfolded. The staff was not entirely happy with this hotshot outsider who had arrived to be their new boss. They complained to the manager that I was trying to turn a three-meal eatery into a haute cuisine gourmet restaurant. I had some backpedaling to do to win their cooperation. But by the end of summer we were working smoothly together.

We did some PR events, especially for a festive promotion we called "Babette's Feast," a takeoff on the recent Academy Award–winning movie. We invited the French consul of Kansas City, various dignitaries, the hotel owner, and others. It was a huge success. That December the media ranked us the number-one restaurant in the city and gave us the Silver Spoon Award.

OVERLOADED

Running an evening restaurant is hard enough on one's family life; being open sixteen hours a day is even worse. I didn't have to be on the job every minute, of course, but it was always on my mind.

The truth is that my wife and kids didn't see much of me during this period. I missed ball games and school programs. My day off was supposed to be Monday, and once in a while I'd take Ben to a video arcade or a matinee movie. If you ask Farah today what I was like as a father, she will say, without malice, "I don't remember much. The truth is, I knew other girls' dads better than my own. We just didn't relate. He was a little closer to Ben than to me—kind of the 'Arab father and son' thing. I was the little sister tagging along, or else just staying home."

> Running an evening restaurant is hard enough on one's family life; being open sixteen hours a day is even worse.

For the family, Sundays were downright boring. Here in the Bible Belt, all the neighbors were at church, it seemed. Our kids had nothing to do but lie around and watch videos. I was gone to the restaurant, of course.

Karen worried about me but was unsure of what to do. I was making good money but paying a high price for it in the quality of life at home. My occasional flare-ups with her grew more frequent and more intense. I'm sure the kids heard us arguing in another room from time to time.

One day, the Westin president and his vice president came by for a talk. They told me that our restaurant had gone from being one of the worst in the chain to the most cost-effective operation out of their 169 units. Customer satisfaction was at a peak. They asked how I had pulled it off, and I told them what I had done.

"Tass," the food and beverage director then said, "we need you in Los Angeles. Our most important hotel is there—the Westin Century Plaza. This is where the president of the United States stays when he comes to LA. If he's not around, his suite goes for six thousand dollars a night.

"Now here's the challenge: We had five stars at this facility once. But we lost one. Apparently there was some slackness in our room service. Will you help us get that fifth star back?"

Wow. Who would have predicted that a refugee kid from the Gaza Strip would rise to these heights? Of course, I said yes to the opportunity.

It didn't seem wise to uproot the whole family for this job, however. I'd be working longer hours than ever. Karen and I weren't having a good time in each other's presence anyway. It was agreed that I would go to Los Angeles alone.

I jumped into the project with both feet. No detail was too small for me to examine. I put my stamp on everything from menus to supplier selection to staff training. A smoking habit I had picked up now accelerated out of control. But after much hard work, we regained our five-star rating the very next year.

I didn't go home to Kansas City very often that year. I was too busy. Besides, I was meeting a variety of interesting women in LA. The thought of going back to Karen wasn't very appealing to me. Whenever I talked with her on the phone, she told stories about how tough it was to make ends meet and how hard single parenting was. I'd say things like, "Well, I'm sending you all the money I can. It's not cheap living in this city, let me tell you." We would end up squabbling about all kinds of things. I began wishing that she would just go ahead and file for divorce. I wanted to split from her but couldn't bring myself to take the first step.

Soon the Westin management decided to reward me with a promotion to general manager of just about any hotel in the chain—I could pretty much take my pick of the openings. Elated, I began looking through the list. But suddenly, before I could make my selection, the travel and lodging industry hit a downturn. Several Westins had to close. My promotion evaporated in the wind.

ACCUSED!

And then I got the shock of my life when Hotel Security called me with bad news: one of our waitresses had filed a sexual harassment complaint against me. She had to be kidding! I racked my brain to figure out what she could have been thinking of. The day before, she and I had walked together through the garden from our building over to the tower. Along the way, she brought up a request for some time off. I told her I wasn't authorized to say yes, but I'd see what could be done. That was it.

But then I remembered that my accuser was dating a guy in Security. Had they teamed up to try to get settlement money from the hotel? This was nuts.

I panicked, fearing this situation could ruin my whole career. The hotel manager was grim as he said to me, "I hope you realize that this could cause us all a lot of problems. You're a manager, not just a minor employee. A scandal could cost Westin a lot of credit in the political community, and a lot of money, too. The police will have to take care of this."

When I showed up at the Santa Monica police station, I was interviewed by a sour-faced female officer. I shivered to think what she could do to me in her report. I started talking fast. "You know, this waitress is definitely 'eye candy.' And to be honest with you, if I wasn't her boss, she's the kind I would go for. But not in the middle of the workplace. Honest, I didn't touch her!

I panicked. This situation could ruin my whole career.

"I'm not saying I'm an angel, you understand? I've played around in the past—I admit it. But not with this one. I didn't make any advances. I didn't invite her to anything. I was entirely professional. Especially because of my job—I'd have been an idiot to make a move on her."

The woman in the uniform slowly raised her eyes from her paperwork. "I don't know why," she said at last, "but for some reason I actually think you're telling me the truth."

"I am! I am!" I fairly shouted at her. "The trouble is, the damage is already done. Everybody thinks I'm guilty."

"Well, I don't," the officer replied. "I questioned this girl, and I didn't believe a word she was saying. So just forget about it. Nothing's going to show up in your record or anybody else's."

I let out a huge sigh. "Really?"

"Just go on with your work and try to turn your back on this. I know she's lying. I'll handle it."

The officer kept her promise. She wrote to the hotel management that I was innocent. I was so relieved.

But the next time I talked with my vice president, I could tell his attitude toward me had changed. I mentioned the earlier promise about a promotion to general manager.

"No, that's not going to work," he responded. "We don't see an opportunity for you to move to a different location. I suppose we could promote you to a slightly higher spot here at this hotel," he said, and he spelled out the details. It was far less than what I had been dreaming of.

I asked for a little time to consider it. "Let me think that over, and I'll get back to you with a decision," I said.

I could instantly tell he wasn't happy with what I had said. "Actually, we've already considered that decision for you," he announced. "Given the circumstances, it would be best if you simply look for another job. Our severance package for you will be quite generous. I'm sure there's a new challenge waiting for you out there in the marketplace. Go for it, Tass!"

The air had just been let out of my high-flying balloon. *What should I do now?*

I tested the job scene in California with other chains and landed one offer, but somehow I didn't feel like starting over there. I opted to shop my résumé back in Kansas City, where I had more connections, and I quickly landed a job offer with the Ritz-Carlton group there. But when I went for my interview with the president, I knew quickly that I could not work for him. His attitude was insufferable as far as I was concerned. I quickly said a no-thank-you and left.

My cash supply was running dangerously low. I wasn't prepared for a long job search. I had blown way too much money in

California on women and nightclubs, assuming that I would always have a job on the upswing. Now I was in trouble.

Meanwhile, Karen had been working two jobs just to put food on our table and pay the rent on the small two-bedroom apartment to which she had downsized us to save money. Desperately I sent out résumés, called my list of contacts, tried to get freelance business—anything to make ends meet. The result: nothing. Silence all around.

As for our kids, I could tell they were more distant than ever. They were now into their teenage years, and they had gotten along somehow without me for over a year. We could spend an entire evening in the same room and never utter a sentence to one another. It seemed they didn't really need me anymore.

GRASPING AT STRAWS

After nine months of struggle, I got a bright idea. Or at least I thought it was bright. How about starting a drive-through restaurant, like those successful In–N-Out burger franchises I had seen in California, only this one would feature Middle Eastern food along with hamburgers? I knew how to make the best *shawarma*—fine-cut meat from a skewer—and *falafel* and other great things. It would be awesome.

I floated the idea to my father. He was willing to send my younger brother over from Qatar to check out the prospects. Based on his report, he would come and help me. We ended up plowing $280,000 into the venture.

The only trouble was, Kansas City folk didn't seem to have a great taste for Middle Eastern cuisine. This was good old American steak country. The customer volume never even came close to breaking even. We had to close our doors in late 1991, only nine months after we had opened. I was more deflated than ever, and Karen and the kids were justifiably worried. Were we going to end up on the street?

Just at that desperate moment in our lives, the phone rang again. It was the owners of La Méditerranée—the French man with the German wife.

"What are you doing these days, Tass?"

"Well, I'm kind of between things at the moment," I said, trying not to reveal too much.

"We've been talking about you here. Business has been a little slow for us recently, and we were wondering if you would be available to get us back on track like before."

"Sounds interesting," I said, trying to control my enthusiasm. "I'm still interested in buying the place, by the way."

"Yes, we know. And in fact, we're willing to sell it to you."

"Okay, let's get together and talk."

The couple was indeed ready to sell this time. But they wanted to stick to the figure I had offered back when the restaurant was going strong, which was more than half a million dollars. I looked at their current books and said, "I don't think so. This place isn't worth that much now." We haggled back and forth a while and finally settled on $275,000. We signed a contract that said I would help them recover the business and then pay the money two years down the road.

It was like déjà vu to jump in and revive La Méditerranée once again. When I walked through the dining room, I realized how much I had missed the place. The walls had been painted light blue, and there were now crystal chandeliers and white tablecloths, so that the dark ambience of the 1980s was gone. But it could be remodeled back to its original state.

I got busy rejuvenating the menu. I taught the waiters how to prepare dishes right at the table, stirring up salads and flambéing entrées. This had always been a great crowd pleaser. We brought in vintage wines, the most expensive of which went up to $1,300 a bottle. Our clientele could afford it, though; we were the playground of Kansas City's high society.

The ownership change was just about to be finalized when we got news that the landlord, with whom the couple had experienced problems, was going to pull our lease. He wanted to put the property to a different use. So in the middle of our rise to prosperous times, we would have to move the restaurant.

"Charlie, what am I going to do about *this*?" I asked my old friend. "We have to get out by March 15. What a mess!"

"Well, let's think about it," he replied, ever the optimistic one. "I'll have some of my people scout around for you. And you be looking, too. It could all work out after all."

We began shopping the possibilities. One Saturday evening in late February, he came in beaming.

"Tass, I've got a surprise for you!"

"What's that?"

"I've found a wonderful building. It's perfect for your restaurant."

"Great! Where is it?"

"Just off Broadway," he answered. "It's a beautiful building just beyond the Japanese place. It's called 'The Villa.'"

The excitement drained from my face. I had already seen this location a few days before, with my own realtor. Nice property— but it was a former mortuary. It gave me the creeps. I couldn't stop thinking about dead bodies in those rooms. . . .

"Charlie, I already saw that place this past week. When I went inside, I got freaked out—it used to be a funeral home! If *I* felt that way, what will the guests feel?"

Charlie just laughed. Then he looked straight into my eyes. In a tender voice I didn't remember hearing in the nineteen years we had known each other, he said, "Tass, do you know why you felt afraid that way?"

"No, why?"

"It's because you don't have the fear of God in you."

What a gutsy thing to say to a friend—especially a Muslim friend! I was a little offended.

"Charlie, what are you saying?" I shot back. "You know I'm a Muslim. I fear God!"

> "You don't have the fear of God in you."

"No, you don't—not really," he replied. "But don't worry; I can help you." And then he pointed his finger toward the ceiling as he said with a twinkle in his eye, "I've got a connection!"

"Yeah, sure," I said with a laugh as I walked away.

CHASING "THE CONNECTION"

The evening wore on, and in quieter moments I thought about Charlie. He was the one who had thanked me long ago for clearing away his dishes. I'd always felt an appreciation for him, even though he was a rich American and I was a Palestinian immigrant. He had been my career adviser over the years, and more than that, my friend.

He had never seemed religious before. But now he was different in a way I couldn't quite identify. In the past few months he had stopped ordering liquor. He seemed more even tempered.

What in the world was this "connection" he spoke about? Did he mean some link to the Mafia? Or something else? For the next three weeks, every time I saw him I would say, "Hey, tell me about your 'connection.' What's that all about?"

"Not now, Tass," he would respond. "You're not ready yet." This only mystified me even more.

The last Saturday night at the old location, March 13, arrived. Once we closed that night, we would be packing up the décor, tableware, and kitchen utensils to move to another place we had still not yet identified. The tension was mounting.

The restaurant was packed that night. All our regular customers, it seemed, wanted to enjoy La Méditerranée one last time. The atmosphere was both joyful and melancholy. Some of the waiters seemed on the verge of tears as they went about their serving.

I stood at the front desk welcoming customers. But I got distracted repeatedly, staring over at Charlie's table. Finally I left my post and went to see him. I knelt down by his chair.

"Charlie, I have to know," I whispered. "What's this 'connection'?"

"What are you doing, Tass?" he asked. "Your guests need you right now, don't they? This place is swarming."

"I don't care," I replied, pleading with him. "I can hardly think about anything else. Tell me, please!" I may have been a forty-two-year-old man running a thriving business, but I sounded like a little kid.

"Okay, I can see that you're ready now," Charlie said. "But not right here. Let's meet tomorrow to talk things over, all right?"

"When?"

"You call me at half past one in the afternoon, and then we'll settle on a time to get together."

The next afternoon, when I dialed Charlie's number, he answered in a cheerful voice, "How are you, Tass?"

"Miserable," I replied honestly.

"What's up?" he asked. "Why is that?"

"I've got to talk to you!"

"Okay, come over to my place," he said.

I told him I was too nervous to drive. This "connection" thing was driving me crazy.

"All right, stay put then," he said. "I'll come pick you up. I'll be there in twenty minutes."

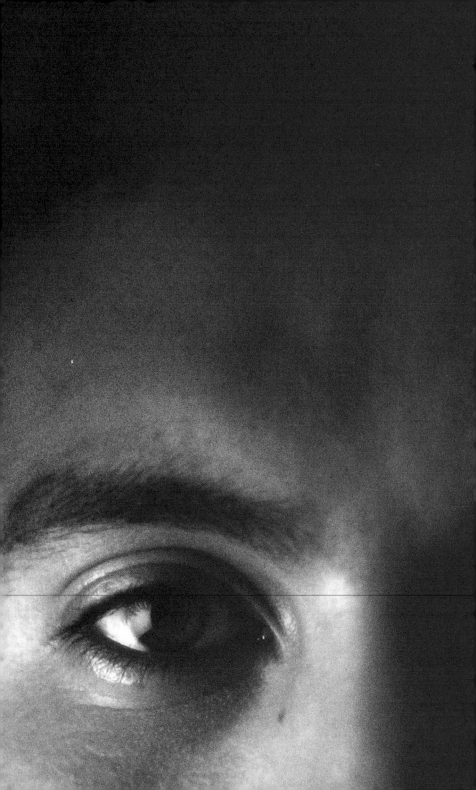

PART 2

HOW
I
LEARNED
TO
LOVE

CHAPTER 10

SURRENDER

CHARLIE SHARPE TALKED NONSTOP as we drove to his house, telling me about the recent change in his life. I didn't understand half of what he was saying, probably because I wasn't paying full attention.

He was still talking as we pulled into the driveway of his large, two-story home in North Kansas City and headed inside. He opened the door for me so I could enter first. All of a sudden, I clued into his words as he said, " . . . So the thing is this, Tass. If you want to have the peace I have, you must love a Jew."

What?!

I froze in my tracks. Why would he say an outrageous thing like that? Charlie knew me very well. He knew about my past with Fatah. He knew I hated Jews with a passion. Was he Jewish, and I hadn't known it all these years?

I swung around with a startled look on my face. "Why would you risk saying something like *that*? Stop it, please!"

"Calm down, man, relax. Come on in and sit down," he replied, gesturing toward the couch in his living room.

I sat down and took an extra breath. I needed to get this

conversation back on track. "Okay, Charlie, what about this 'connection' thing? What have you been talking about these past weeks?"

"Well," he said, "for starters, tell me what you know about Jesus Christ."

"He was a prophet. We Muslims respect and honor him for that. In fact, he was one of the most important prophets."

"Actually, he's more than a prophet," Charlie said. "He is God's son. He's the only God."

I bristled instantly. "That really makes me angry," I responded. "What you just said is blasphemy." To Muslims, the idea of God's having a son implies that God had sex with Mary, which is a horrible thought.

I stood up to leave. "I don't know what's wrong with you," I continued. "First you told me I didn't have the fear of God in me; now today you've said I have to love a Jew and that Jesus is supposed to be God's son. This is nonsense. I'm out of here."

"If you want to have the peace I have, you must love a Jew."

"Just a minute," he countered, raising one hand. "Give me a chance to explain myself, all right? You haven't heard what I'm really wanting to say."

Out of respect for our long friendship, I sat back down again. He picked up a book and placed it on the couch between us. I looked and saw it was a Bible.

Immediately I jumped up and away from it.

"What's wrong?" Charlie wanted to know.

"I must not touch that book!"

"Why not? It's just paper."

"No!" I disagreed. "It's God's Word!"

He looked at me in surprise. "Do you really believe that?"

"Yes, I do."

Now in saying this, I wasn't following clear Muslim teaching. The truth is, at that moment even I couldn't quite figure out the words coming from my mouth. The conversation was growing surreal.

"Well, if you believe that," Charlie said, "then let me read you what God's Word says about Jesus Christ. Fair enough?"

I nodded.

He picked up this Bible, a brand-new one with a blue leather binding, and opened it at random. He began to read: "In the beginning was the Word, and the Word was with God, and the Word was God."* He had not chosen this passage on purpose; the Bible just fell open to that place.

The instant he said, "Word," I began to shake. He thought he was just reading a verse of Christian Scripture. He had no idea that the Qur'an clearly says, "The Messiah, Jesus son of Mary, was . . . the Messenger of God, and *His Word* that He committed to Mary, and a *Spirit* from Him."† Hearing the Bible say essentially the same thing, that Jesus was the Word of God, struck deep to the core of my being.

BURST OF LIGHT

Before I knew it, I was on my knees. I didn't consciously *decide* to kneel; it just happened. I lost all awareness that Charlie was even in the room. A light came into my field of vision—a talking light. Now I know this sounds really odd, and readers may say I was hallucinating. I can only tell you how events unfolded that afternoon on Sunday, March 14, 1993.

The light said in an audible tone, "I am the way and the truth and the life. No one comes to the Father except through me." I didn't know at that moment that these words were a repetition of what Jesus said during the Last Supper.‡ As far as I was concerned, they were a message from Jesus solely to me.

Then, just beside the light, I saw a pair of hands folded in prayer. On the back of one of the hands, a cross had been tattooed. Instantly I thought of my childhood nanny, a young Filipino woman who worked for our family. Her name was Maryam. She had had the

---

*John 1:1
†Sura (chapter) 4:171, italics added
‡John 14:6

very same cross on her hand. I had not seen her since I was ten years old, when we moved from Jiddah to Qatar. Yet I knew beyond any doubt that I was once again looking at her hands.

The light said in an audible tone, "I am the way and the truth and the life."

In this indescribable moment, I knew something else: the triune God existed—Father, Son, and Holy Spirit. I knew that this God loved me. "Oh, Jesus, come into my life!" I blurted out. "Forgive me and be my Lord and Savior!" I felt as if a heavy load went flying off my shoulders. A sense of peace and joy rushed into my heart. The presence of God was so real it seemed I could almost reach out and touch it.

I opened my eyes to see Charlie on his knees beside me. We were both crying by then.

"What's going on?" I said to him at last. "What happened?"

He could barely talk. "Never in my life have I seen something like this," he said. "I read one sentence from the Bible, and you started shaking. Then you were lifted up off the sofa and dropped onto your knees. Your hands went up. . . . Then you said something I didn't understand. It wasn't in English." He shook his head in wonder.

"Well, whatever happened must be something good," I said. "I've never felt better in my life."

To affirm this unexpected and somewhat mystical experience of mine, he quickly explained an essential fact. "The Bible says that 'there is no other name under heaven given to men by which we must be saved,'"* Charlie explained. He then led me in a prayer of salvation. I repeated the words after him:

> Lord Jesus, I am a sinner, and I am sorry for my sin. I ask you to forgive me and wash away my sin by your precious blood. Lord, I can't save myself. I can't take away my sin, but you can. You are the Savior of the world—the only Savior—and I want you to be my Savior.

*Acts 4:12

I ask you to forgive me and come into my life. Change me and give me a new heart. I will forever love you and follow you.

Now I thank you for hearing my prayer and saving my soul. I know you have, because you promised you would. Now I am yours, and you are mine. I will serve you the rest of my life.

This prayer served to nail down the important reality of what had happened a few minutes earlier. I am well aware that not everyone's conversion to faith in Jesus Christ is quite so spectacular or dramatic. But a high percentage of Muslims who come to faith in Christ do so because of a vision, dream, or other supernatural experience. I believe this is not because we are something special but because we are stubborn. Others who convert simply because they hear the gospel and believe are perhaps the most blessed. Their conversion events can be highly cerebral as they accept the essential facts of the gospel in their minds, and later on it touches their hearts and emotions.

For me, I can only tell you my experience. Yes, it was unusual, surprising, almost bizarre. But it was nevertheless real. The phrase "born again" fit my reality perfectly. I felt as if I were starting life all over again.

Charlie gave me a Bible before driving me back that day. I was overwhelmed with joy and peace. Along the way, I pulled my pack of cigarettes and my lighter out of my pocket. I hadn't had a cigarette the whole afternoon—a highly unusual thing for a six-pack-a-day smoker. Now I looked at these things in my hand and said to myself, *I'm not going to need these anymore.*

I opened the window of Charlie's car and threw them out right there. "What are you doing?" he asked me, surprised. He knew how entrenched my smoking habit had become.

"All this time with you, I haven't had one cigarette," I said. "Guess I don't need them anymore."

"That's fantastic, Tass!" he responded. "Hallelujah!" I didn't exactly know what that word meant, but it sounded like a happy thing.

He dropped me off at the restaurant, where a number of my staff were working to clean up. I nearly floated from place to place. I wasn't really in touch with the details of what they were doing.

Karen and the kids were there as well. I told my wife in passing, "Guess what—I think I've become a Christian." She just laughed. By now, my wife had learned not to take seriously a lot of what I said.

THE MOST UNLIKELY PRAYER

When I awoke the next day, Monday morning, Karen was already in the kitchen. For some reason, I slid down onto my knees by the bed right away. I wanted to pray. But big tears began streaming from my eyes.

"O God, I thank you for everything you're doing in my life," I prayed aloud. "Thank you for the joy. Thank you for the peace. You are the true God. I love you!" At this, I wept even more.

And then I heard myself praying something totally out of character for me. "O God, bless your people Israel. O Lord, lead them back to their Promised Land. Let them see you as their God."

What was this?!

I clapped my hand over my mouth. I had never wished a single good thing for the Jews in my entire life. Why was I now praying for their interests? I had no explanation for the inner urge I felt to ask blessings upon them. It made no sense.

I picked up the bedroom phone and called Charlie. "I cannot believe what I just prayed, spontaneously," I said. "Why would I pray something like this? Tell me, is Jesus a Jew?"

"Yes, he is!" came the boisterous reply through the phone.

That was the last thing I wanted to hear. I started getting upset. What was happening to my identity as a Jew-hating Palestinian? But I had come to love Jesus. So where did that leave me in relation to his Jewishness?

I have an awful lot to learn, don't I? I said to myself.

I went looking for the Bible Charlie had given me. On the way, I passed the main bathroom. My son, Ben, then almost nineteen years old, was shaving.

"Hi, Son!" I said with uncharacteristic enthusiasm. He looked up at me, white shaving cream spread across his face.

"I want to share something with you," I continued.

"What is it, Dad?"

"Yesterday I . . . I invited Jesus Christ into my heart. I think I've become a Christian."

Ben stared at me for a few seconds, his eyes growing wider. Then suddenly he rushed to hug me. Shaving cream smeared across my neck. I could feel his body start to shake with tears. That made me start crying, too.

"Dad, I'm so happy for you!" he finally said.

An unusual comment. "Why is that?" I asked.

He composed himself enough to answer. "Just three months ago, I became a Christian myself. But I've been afraid to tell you."

The story came out that his girlfriend of three years, a Christian, had finally decided to break up with him because their beliefs just didn't match. He knew she loved him regardless. He could tell this was a very hard move for her to make.

"So what do you believe?" he had asked her. "How can I learn more about it?"

That led him to start going with her to her church, the five-thousand-member Kansas City Baptist Temple. There he had heard the gospel clearly explained. Finally one night at her house, she put the question to him directly: "What are you thinking, Ben? Are you going to make a decision to follow Jesus, or not?"

I clapped my hand over my mouth. I had never wished a single good thing for the Jews in my entire life.

My son had not answered her directly. But he came home to his room that night—and there he gave his heart to Christ. He began walking the new path of a person who loves Jesus. He got a Bible, but he was afraid I would find it. So he read it only late at night in his room, then hid it under his bed.

At one point, he had gone to an associate pastor and said, "My father is a Muslim. What should I do? If he finds out I've become a Christian, he'll kill me." That fear was overblown as far as I was concerned, but to Ben it was real.

"Go home, love your dad more than you ever did before, and leave the rest to God," the pastor advised.

He then said to a large Bible study at the church, "We have a burden we must carry together. A boy from a Muslim family has accepted Jesus, and he's afraid that if his dad finds out, he might do something violent. We need to pray for this father." They even organized a round-the-clock prayer chain for Ben's home situation.

How interesting that during those three months, I became intrigued with Charlie Sharpe's "connection" to God. A coincidence? I don't think so.

SKEPTICAL WIFE

Karen said later that she had begun noticing a change in Ben; he seemed more mature, more cooperative, and more respectful. But when she heard my outlandish story of what had happened at Charlie's house—the light, the praying hands, the emotional upheaval—she waved it off. Just another one of her husband's crazy escapades, she thought. After all, she was the one in the house with a Christian heritage, and it certainly had never taken on any outbursts like that. God was much too dignified to trigger that kind of reaction. And if I were just pretending to be a Christian, that surely would not sit well with the Almighty. He would not tolerate that kind of fooling around, she told me.

In the back of her mind, she was wondering if Charlie had either promised me money or given me a job—especially in light of the restaurant's transition. If, for the second time in two years, I wound up without a job, Charlie would have an even bigger influence over me, she surmised. Maybe I was saying I was a Christian in order to get on Charlie's good side. I tried to convince her that I had genuinely given my life to Christ of my own free will, but I didn't get very far.

That first Monday I had begun digging into the Bible for myself. I started at the beginning, in the book of Genesis. I read about how

God created Adam. I visualized the action of God kneeling down in the dirt and forming a man's body. I thought about God smiling as he said to himself, "Good! This is beautiful." And then he bent even lower to put his lips on Adam's face, breathing into his nostrils. And Adam twitched. . . .

I stopped reading to savor this incredible image. I began weeping again.

My tears were not just out of joy that God had created a living, breathing human being. They were also tears of remorse as I thought about how many human beings I had blown away with my sniper's rifle. I had studied them through my telescopic sight. There they were, made in the image of God. And then I had pulled the trigger.

"Oh God, I killed those people you had created!" I sobbed. "I don't think I should live anymore. Open up the ground and swallow me! I deserve to die for what I did!" My chest heaved with the awful weight of my wickedness.

And then came a voice in my ear: "Even that, I have forgiven."

Peace began to return to my soul. God was not holding my sins on a scale to see if my good deeds would outweigh them, as I had been taught in Islam. He had totally, completely forgiven me. I was overwhelmed by the thought of his mercy.

I kept reading the next day, and the next, and the next. I had extra time now, since there was only so much I could do in searching for a new restaurant location. Between site visits with the realtor and the French chef, I had hours to give to my new exploration of the Word of God. I began understanding things I had never known before.

About a week passed. I was sitting in the living room reading my Bible, and through the door I could see Karen cooking dinner in the kitchen. The smell was wonderful. She stopped to add another dish to the oven. I got to thinking about how long we had been together—nineteen years. She had always been a good wife. She had done a great job as the mother of our children. She had stuck with me through hard times as well as prosperous ones.

She had remained with me even when she knew I was cheating on her.

I thought about the many times over the years that she had said, "I love you, Tass," and the only honest response I could muster was, "Well, thank you." I could never bring myself to lie by going further.

Now as I watched her cook, a feeling of genuine love began to well up within me. My heart began to beat faster. This was really an amazing woman. I needed to let her know that I truly did value her. I needed to drop the aloofness and let my new affection express itself.

I stood up and moved toward the kitchen. "Karen!" I said. "You know what? I really do love you."

She calmly went on with her cooking. She didn't even turn around for a while. I waited. Eventually, she looked up in my direction. Her face was a mask.

"All right, Tass—what do you want?"

In that moment, I felt like the football coach at the end of the game when his players dump a chest of ice water over his head. She didn't believe me.

But then—why should she? I had sown so much doubt and suffering into her heart over the years. Our life together had always been about my wishes, my career, my ideas. She had figured out by now that in the beginning our marriage had been only a ploy on my part to get a green card. In fact, I had admitted that to her at one point. So I couldn't blame her now.

I answered her question by saying, "I'm not asking for anything. I just wanted to say that I love you. I hope that's okay. . . ."

She replied, "Well, I guess so. It's just that you've never told me that before!"

I couldn't deny that fact. We let the conversation go at that moment. I simply determined in my heart to show her over time that I now truly cared about her. I asked the Lord to mend our relationship as only he could do.

My daughter, Farah, wasn't buying this "new dad" thing at all.

At fifteen and a half, she was suspicious. She had learned to get along without me all these years, and now whenever I reached out to her, she seemed to pull away. What could I do to win back her trust and affection?

Over the next six weeks or so, I kept reading the Bible and praying to God for guidance on how to repair my family. Charlie and a wise pastor gave good input into my life. I saw that I had a lot to confess to Karen. I poured out my heart to her about all my past indiscretions, and I asked for her forgiveness.

She began to take me seriously. When she noticed me getting out of bed in the middle of the night to pray, she told herself I wasn't just putting on an act. Farah, as well, thought it was odd to see me reading something other than the sports section of the newspaper. She saw me time and again with a Bible and a yellow highlighter in my hand. She noticed when I was tender with Karen—when I would hold her hand while driving in the car—and she said to herself that something was definitely different about her dad.

Karen got connected with a caring mentor named Shirley, a mature woman who helped her identify the many frustrations and hardships she harbored in her memory. They prayed together many times about the pain and rejection she had endured all throughout her adult life. God worked to relieve her of these weights.

The healing process took a while, and I tried not to rush her. In time she was able to say, "Tass, I forgive you. I love you. Our past life is over. Let's begin a new one, okay?"

We began reading the Bible together. I was learning so many new things, and I excitedly shared them with her. At first she was a little put off, thinking, *Look who's teaching whom! I'm supposed to receive Bible knowledge from this former philanderer who didn't even grow up in church like I did?* But she quickly got past this viewpoint. We both submitted ourselves to the Word of God. We wanted to learn everything we could that would help us.

On Sunday morning, April 18, 1993, at New Life Community Church, Karen stepped forward at the end of the service to publicly commit her life to Christ. She had always been a good person, and of course she had a church background. But now she wanted to make a personal profession of faith. I watched with joy and thankfulness in my heart. We were restarting our life together on a whole new foundation.

CHAPTER 11

NEW DAY

AS I READ FARTHER IN THE BOOK OF GENESIS, I was surprised by what was missing. I didn't find much in the early chapters about Jews. In fact, I had to get all the way to chapter 32 before reaching the story of how God changed Jacob's name to Israel. Even then it was simply this one man's name for the rest of the book. Not until the next book, Exodus, did the Bible start talking about Israelites as a clan or ethnic group.

Long before then, I had run into some fascinating information about *my* people, the Palestinians. Our ancestor, I knew, was Ishmael—the firstborn son of Abram. Ishmael's mother was Hagar, the Egyptian servant whom Abram had no doubt acquired during his and his wife Sarai's short stay in that country.

I had heard of at least some Christians who called Ishmael everything from a bastard to a brat, and had even nastier things to say about his mother. But that is not what I read in the actual Bible. Here I read that the elderly couple, desperate for an heir, invited Hagar into the marriage. Sarai specifically "gave her to her husband *to be his wife*," it said.* Nothing downplayed Hagar as a concubine,

---

*Genesis 16:3, italics added

a temptress, or a one-night stand. She was, by common agreement, a fully validated wife. Any children would be entirely legitimate according to the customs of that day.

When tensions arose during Hagar's pregnancy, so much so that she fled into the desert, she was not left to fend for herself. No less than "the angel of the LORD"* came to her aid. Who was this heavenly being? I did some research and found out that many commentators view this as an early appearance of Christ—the first in human history that we know of. What an honor for my ancestral mother!

The angel instructed her to go back home and then promised, "I will so increase your descendants that they will be too numerous to count."† I leaned back in my chair and thought of all the people who trace back to this woman—not just us Palestinians, but all the Arabs. What a massive population we had become, just as the divine messenger had predicted!

Soon the angel was even telling Hagar the gender of her unborn child ("You will have a son") and what to name him ("You shall name him Ishmael, for the LORD has heard of your misery"‡). Indeed, I knew the Arabic word *ishma* even today means "to hear." This was, in fact, God's debut into the business of naming (or renaming) people, a practice he would carry on later with such important figures as Abram, Sarai, Jacob, Jesus, and Simon the fisherman. But Ishmael was the first to get a God-picked name.

> I had heard of at least some Christians who called Ishmael everything from a bastard to a brat, and had even nastier things to say about his mother. But that is not what I read in the actual Bible.

Hagar obeyed the Lord's messenger that day. She didn't resist or ignore the instruction, even if she harbored fears about returning to Sarai's house. She proved herself to be a willing follower of God.

* Genesis 16:7
† Genesis 16:10
‡ Genesis 16:11

Soon the baby was born. Abram, from everything we can tell, was a proud father. This was the fulfillment of his long-awaited dream. No doubt he poured great amounts of time and resources into his growing boy. In the previous chapter, God had said to Abram, "To your descendants I give this land, from the river of Egypt to the great river, the Euphrates."* Now that Abram had a son, whom would he naturally assume to be in line for all this land? Ishmael, obviously—there was no one else to point to, and there wouldn't be for another thirteen years.

By chapter 17, God was setting up a covenant with Abram. He decided to change his name to Abraham, which reflected a new life purpose for this man: "father of many nations."† Not just one nation, but *many.* Yes, the Jews would turn out to be one of those nations. But not the only one.

When God began talking about a second son to be born, with Sarah as the mother this time, Abraham quickly rose to his firstborn's defense. You can feel his fatherly devotion as he says to God, "If only Ishmael might live under your blessing!"‡ It's almost as if he's saying, "Oh, but . . . but . . . please, God, I already have a son. He's my pride and joy. You're not going to bypass him, are you? Surely not!"

And God quickly allays his fear by answering, "As for Ishmael, I have heard you: I will surely bless him; I will make him fruitful and will greatly increase his numbers. He will be the father of twelve rulers, and I will make him into a great nation."§

When I read those words, I just about came out of my chair. So we Arabs were *not* cursed by God after all! We were not, as so many people think, the scum of the human race. The one God, the only true and living God, is the God of the Ishmaelites, too. Yes, Isaac would come along later, and his descendants would play a special role in God's plan. But their position as the chosen people did not erase the promises of Genesis 15–17. God had already put himself on record to bless the offspring of Abraham and Hagar.

---

*Genesis 15:18
†Genesis 17:5
‡Genesis 17:18
§Genesis 17:20

I was feeling prouder of my heritage all the time, thanks to what I saw here in the Old Testament. The *Christian* book (actually, the *Jewish-Christian* book) was building up my self-esteem as an Arab! Who would have expected that?

THE NEW TASS

My immediate job these days, of course, was to find a new home for La Méditerranée. As soon as I could nail this down, the ownership of the restaurant would pass over to me, and my longtime dream would become reality.

I was out with a realtor one day looking at a property that held some potential. The moment I met the seller, I saw that he was Jewish. We began negotiating. My policy in such situations in the past had always been, "Sack him for lunch before he eats you for dinner." I knew how to be a tough bargainer—especially with Jews.

But as I sat there talking with this man, I realized there was no more fight left in me. I had no desire to fleece him. A quiet joy came over my spirit, along with a touch of surprise. This wasn't the way I had always operated in the business world. But it felt right. It was part of what the Bible meant when it talked about being a "new creation; the old has gone, the new has come!"*

To my amazement, the seller sat there and was quite agreeable. The negotiation was entirely pleasant. Charlie Sharpe had told me I would find peace if I would learn to love a Jew. The Jew, Jesus Christ, had drained out of me my long-standing hatred for all other Jews. These people were no longer my foes. They were instead my cousins, going back to Abraham. I began to see that the closer we all got to Jesus, the Messiah, the more reconciled we could become to one another. My heart had been cleansed of its anger.

I began enthusiastically telling my Arab friends around Kansas City about the Jesus I had discovered. Some of them, in fact, were former employees of mine. I felt a deep passion to show them the truth about Jesus and what he could do for us Arabs.

My fervor was probably greater than my wisdom. They knew I

*2 Corinthians 5:17

had fought with Fatah in the past, and now they said, "You know what, Tass? You've always been fired up about something. That's kind of your style. We've heard about other people who, when they get right down to the edge of life, they turn to Jesus. But for us—no, thank you. We're Muslim, and we're going to stay Muslim."

One guy even said he was afraid of me. He thought that if he didn't convert to Christianity, I might kill him!

> The Jew, Jesus Christ, had drained out of me my long-standing hatred for all other Jews.

"No, that's not true at all," I told him. "There are lots of Palestinians in the Middle East who follow Jesus. Even George Habash, who founded the PFLP, is a Greek Orthodox Christian. So it's not impossible."

My Muslim friends remained skeptical, no doubt because my presentation wasn't the best. The same thing happened when we told Karen's parents. I thought they would be happy that I had finally come over to "their side" of things. They, however, had gotten comfortable with Islam, calling it "a good religion." They didn't see the point of my changing. Karen and I could sense an increased distance whenever we were with them. I was no longer the party guy son-in-law who would drink the evening away with them and tell racy stories.

They were pleased, however, that I seemed more attentive to their daughter now, as well as faithful to her. They gave me credit for that much.

CUT OFF

Meanwhile, what should I say to *my* parents back in Qatar?

I sat down and handwrote a seven-page letter—a remarkable achievement for me. I tried as best I could to explain what had happened in my life. I outlined the differences between Islam and Christianity. I told them I still loved them and simply wanted to share what was going on in my heart.

I tried out the letter on Karen and the kids before sending it.

They listened as I translated my sentences into English. "That's amazing," my wife said when I finished. "The Holy Spirit must have really helped you with that."

I knew I was taking a risk, but I wanted my family to hear it directly from me, instead of someone else. Converting to another religion is an enormous scandal in the Islamic world. It befouls the family honor as badly as adultery. So I held my breath as I mailed the letter and waited for a response.

It didn't take long. Back came twenty-one pages, inscribed by one of my brothers on behalf of the whole family. Its essence was this: "You are crazy. If you don't come back to Islam immediately, we will kill you at the first chance we get."

Of course, there was no practical way for them to reach me here on the other side of the Atlantic. To do me harm on American soil would be a crime. Nevertheless, it was a sobering threat to receive. It grieved me that the family fabric now had a giant rip in it.

I tried to reason with them during subsequent phone calls. My father picked up the line one time and shouted, "Now you worship a piece of wood! How disgusting. And three gods!"

"No, Father, that is not true," I responded. "The cross is a symbol—but we don't worship it. It only represents the death of our Lord and Savior Jesus Christ.

"You are crazy. If you don't come back to Islam immediately, we will kill you at the first chance we get."

"And no, there are not three gods. There is only one God, Almighty, who manifests himself in three persons. After all, he is God—he can do whatever he likes. If he wants to be born as a baby to a woman in a stable, he can do so, right? Why should we force him into a tight category that only suits our limited thinking?"

I went on to say to my father that I had lived here in America a long time now, doing every sin imaginable according to just about any religion. I had lived without boundaries. I drank (which is a total taboo in Islam), chased women, and hurt my associates. "But none of you ever reproached me for this. None of you ever said, 'Tass, you are living in sin. You need to stop it!'

"Now I have pledged myself to straighten up, take care of my family, and help the poor. Why are you upset with me *now*?"

My father would not answer. He simply said, "As long as you live, we will have nothing to do with you." He then hung up the phone.

I kept calling back. No one would take my call. I had been entirely cut off. I could talk only to God about my parents and siblings, asking him to deal with them on my behalf.

A HOUSE DIVIDED?

Our teenage daughter, Farah, wasn't that much happier with me, although she was respectful about it. Not that she practiced the Islamic faith herself. However, as a sophomore in high school, she drew part of her identity from the fact that she was the only Muslim girl on campus, with an Arab-looking face. Now in a short amount of time her brother, her father, and her mother had all gone a different route.

She was willing to attend church with us on Sundays if we persisted, although she sat coldly through the services. The drive across the city took a long time, and Karen and I talked about moving closer. But that would rip Farah out of her school. "Let's not mess up her life any more than we already have," I said to my wife. "If we want to lead her to Christ, we need to go easy on her."

Then a year after my conversion, in the spring of 1994, the church's youth group was going to a large rally an hour away up in St. Joseph, Missouri, called "Acquire the Fire." They invited Farah to come along. Surprisingly, she agreed.

When we picked her up late that night and were driving home, she spoke up from the backseat. "Mom, Dad," she said, "you know what? It's time we moved closer to church. Jesus is more important than my friends at school."

"What?!" I exclaimed. "What happened to you?"

She began telling all about the evening. She described the music, the speaker, and how God had opened her heart to his love. The ice was broken at last. She wanted to follow the same Jesus we had come to know and value.

In the days that followed, I could only fall on my knees and thank God for uniting all four of us in his purpose. This was a remarkable thing, I knew. It didn't turn out this way for everyone. The fact that we could now pray together as a family and talk freely about the Lord and the Scripture was a marvelous blessing.

A little later that year, the whole family was excited when God somehow gave me the power to drop my smoking habit. Yes, I had thrown my cigarettes out of Charlie's car that first day, thinking I was instantly finished with them. Well, it wasn't quite that easy. I did cut down to less than one pack a day, and I was embarrassed to smoke in public. I especially hid my habit from Charlie, who never said a word about it. But I was not too happy about being a deceiver.

Finally I said to the Lord, "If you want me to stop smoking, you will have to take it away from me. I will not hide anymore. I will smoke publicly." The very next cigarette I lit choked me so bad I was coughing for a long time afterward. Since then, I have never had another cigarette.

Karen and the kids had hated my smoking. It bothered Ben all the time, but he never said anything about it. Karen got headaches from the smoke but for years would not say anything, either, for fear of sending me into a rage.

When I finally quit, I did not want to announce it too soon for fear I would relapse, but eventually the family figured it out. That was a joyful day for us all.

I was also able, as time went by, to be more open with them about my past. I didn't drag them through every gruesome detail of the Fatah years, but I did express my sorrow over the lives I had taken. I said what the Lord was reinforcing in my personal times of Bible reading and meditation: that a human life is not a cheap thing. God cares about every person on this planet, regardless of their affiliation or their actions. He wants to bring them into his arms of love and concern.

For many years, I had repressed my memories of war. The battle at al-Karameh, I told myself, was a great breakthrough for our movement, and it was a kill-or-be-killed situation. Then I would quickly change my attention to some other topic. I didn't want to deal with what actually happened there.

Now I felt awful as I thought about those whom I had cut off prematurely from the chance to be reconciled with God. I begged God to forgive me. And he assured me that he had. But it was hard to forgive myself. When you have erased a human life, you never quite forget it. Remorse keeps coming back, and you have to ask God again and again to assure you that you are pardoned.

WHAT NOW?

Whenever my mind turned from the past to the future, I puzzled over what I really should be doing. Did God want me to continue being a restaurateur for the rest of my life? The hours were long and the demands intense. I wasn't afraid to keep working hard. But was this my true calling in life?

I felt inside that God had other things in mind for me. Getting control of La Méditerranée had been a driving passion of my life for years. It had almost been my god. But now I had a new and true God to serve. I went to the owner couple and shocked them by saying, "I think I do not want to move ahead with the purchase of this restaurant after all. I think it is not the right thing that God wants for my future."

> I wasn't afraid to keep working hard. But was this my true calling in life?

"But you've been after us to sell it to you for a very long time!"

"Yes, that is correct. But things are different now," I replied.

They looked at each other, perplexed. Then they said, "Well, will you stay another two years until we find a new location and train a successor? We want the transition to be smooth."

"Yes, I'm willing to do that," I said. This would give me time to keep learning as a new Christian and keep praying about God's direction in our lives.

Along the way came the opportunity to open a smaller coffee shop in a historic old downtown Kansas City building across from the federal courthouse. It would serve pastries, croissants, sandwiches, and other things just for breakfast and lunch. Karen and I prayed about it and sensed a green light to move ahead. We named it "Café Demi-Tass," after the small cups you use for espresso. (It didn't hurt that my nickname, Tass, was part of the title!)

This place was the smallest eatery I had ever attempted to run, but it turned out to be the most profitable. We dedicated it to the Lord's uses, and it became something of an evangelistic ministry. A dentist in the same building got acquainted with us and eventually gave his heart to the Lord. We began offering prayer times in our café, and many people were touched and encouraged by these.

But by 1995, I knew for certain that the restaurant business would not be my life's work from then on. God seemed to be hinting at something different. Neither Karen nor I was sure what that would be. We earnestly wanted to stay attuned, however, to his leading.

CHAPTER 12

FARMING
LESSONS

IT'S A GOOD THING I DIDN'T KNOW in advance what the next few
years of God's training and shaping would be like. I certainly would
not have signed up for such an experience ahead of time.

All I knew was that Charlie had big dreams for the northeast
corner of Missouri, where he had been born and had grown up on
a farm. He had long wanted me to come see the place of his roots,
but I'd never gotten around to it. Now he was building a Christian
community out there in the middle of the cornfields, he said, to
grow crops, run a cattle operation, and use the proceeds to support
a school for troubled kids who needed a place to go. There would
also be a treatment program for adults with drug addictions. In
the center of everything would be a church. He was going to call it
"Heartland," he said, not only because it was in the middle of the
country but also because it would deal with the deepest issues of
the human heart.

It sounded interesting—for Charlie, that is. He had always been
a fountain of novel ideas.

In late 1995, he invited my wife and me to come so I could
give my testimony at the church there. He even arranged for his

125

personal plane to take us. We took off from Kansas City's down-town airport one Saturday morning and landed half an hour later in the middle of nowhere. Charlie and his wife, Laurie, were there to meet us as we stepped off the plane.

The odor of a barnyard smacked me in the face. "Charlie, what in the world is that smell?" I said, covering my nose.

He beamed from ear to ear. "Tass, that is the fragrance of money!" he explained.

"Well, it smells pretty nasty to me," I replied.

We spent the day following Charlie around, observing his excite-ment about the future of this place. The school's foundation was already in the ground, along with the beginnings of two residences. Charlie got up on a bulldozer and smoothed out the dirt road him-self. I could tell he was energized by it all.

We went to lunch in a small town called La Belle, eating in a humble ma-and-pa restaurant. "Tass, I want you to know," said Charlie, "that I've brought you to the best restaurant in town!" I knew this was a hint to me that maybe I should think about raising the standard in these parts.

That afternoon, we toured his farm and cattle operation. The next morning, we worshiped together with about fifty people from the area, and I spoke about what God had done in my life. Then we flew back to Kansas City. Our trip to the countryside was over quickly.

Early the next Sunday morning, however, a most unusual thing happened. Both Karen and I awakened shortly after three o'clock. Neither one of us could get back to sleep. We finally got up and had coffee.

"What are you thinking about?" my wife asked me over the kitchen table.

"Well, to be honest with you—Heartland," I answered.

"That's very interesting," she responded. "I can't think of any-thing else, either."

"Since we're already awake . . . why don't we drive out there for church today?" I proposed. It was a crazy idea, to go all that distance—two hundred miles—but why not?

So we got dressed and hit the road. Charlie was the most surprised man in the world when he saw us coming across the parking lot around nine o'clock that morning. "What are you two doing here?" he called.

"We just thought we'd come out and worship with you all today."

"Great! Come on in!"

We enjoyed the service that day, spent time in the afternoon with Charlie and Laurie, and then made the long drive back home in the evening.

The next Sunday, we did the same. And the next. And the next.

Charlie came to see me one day at Café Demi-Tass. He said, "You folks are crazy, you know? It's such a long way to drive each week for church."

"Yes. But for some reason we just feel the need to be there."

"So then why don't you move there and help me make the project happen?" he suggested. "I've got all kinds of things that need doing."

"Oh, no, we've got the café here," I said. "Plus, our kids are here." Ben and Farah were both just entering young adulthood by this time. "We couldn't move."

"Well, pray about it, will you?" Charlie said.

COW COUNTRY

We took his request seriously, and the more we prayed about it over a period of time, the more we came to realize that we belonged at Heartland. Why? We really didn't know. But it seemed to be the place where God wanted us.

One Saturday morning, I got up before dawn and drove out to the complex again, all by myself this time. I wrestled with my feelings the whole way. I turned up the gravel road and parked alongside the small lake that served as a centerpiece for the Heartland property. The minute I opened the car door, the smell of manure hit me once again, but I ignored it this time.

It was about 10:30 when I walked to the water's edge and knelt under a big oak tree. I began to pray.

"God, why in the world do I feel so drawn to this place? It's a farm! You know my desire to reach Muslims and Jews with the good news of your peace. Well, I sure don't see any Muslims out here. I don't see any Jews, either. All I see is cows!

"So why should Karen and I come here? You need to show me. . . ."

I prayed for a good length of time beneath that tree, crying as I went along. Then I began to experience something like a vision. I saw myself helping to train young men and women in the food service business. That would help them have a livelihood when they finished the program here at Heartland. Things were starting to make sense after all. I returned home that evening to say, "Karen, I now know that we definitely belong at Heartland. Here is what God showed me today. . . ."

> "God, why in the world do I feel so drawn to this place? I sure don't see any Muslims out here. I don't see any Jews, either. All I see is cows!"

She listened, and then replied, "Really? I haven't heard anything from God yet."

"Okay. Then we'll just wait," I said.

Karen had been taking classes at Longview Community College for her teaching certificate. Suddenly the pieces came together in her mind. She could be a teacher at Heartland!

When Charlie asked us again if we wanted to join the Heartland staff, we were both ready to say yes. He was thrilled. "The only thing is, we have to sell Café Demi-Tass first," I added.

"That won't be a problem," he predicted, ever the optimist. "If the Lord wants you to move, he'll take care of the details."

We put an ad in a small local Christian newspaper. Nobody responded for two months. We got a little discouraged. Then a young man and his wife got in touch with us. They'd been looking for a restaurant opportunity. He said his dad had been flipping through the old newspaper just before throwing it out—and had seen our ad.

These were Christian people who already volunteered in youth work at their Baptist church. So they immediately understood the ministry angle of the café.

They didn't have the amount of cash I was asking for the place, however. Their bank wasn't eager to loan them money for a venture this uncertain. In that moment, I felt what I thought was an inner leading from the Lord: *Finance it yourself, Tass.*

"Lord, how can I do that? I need the cash myself!"

I began praying about it, and in time, the Lord's direction was clarified. What he wanted me to do was not to finance it myself but to help them get financing by cosigning their loan. So that is what happened. I helped them find a lender, signed all the paperwork, and handed over the café keys. Then we packed up and moved to Heartland on January 1, 1997.

BACK TO THE BOTTOM

Karen immediately jumped into teaching fourth through sixth grades in the fledgling school the next year. I spent time working with the rehab program for addicts and alcoholics. These young men were hired to help run the dairy operation that was just taking shape. It was good discipline for them and also helped to generate operating cash.

Within a couple of weeks, I was feeling awfully cut off from the city life I had enjoyed for so long. This was definitely not Los Angeles, nor even Kansas City. The village of Newark a few miles north had 122 people. If I drove the other direction, I'd come to Bethel—population 103! The nearest city of any size was Quincy, Illinois, nearly an hour's drive east across the Mississippi River. Even there, I wasn't likely to run into any Arabs or Muslims.

I tried to concentrate on my most natural interest, which was the school kitchen. I quickly found out that I would *not* be in charge. There was already a director of food service, a woman who was practically clueless about how to run this kind of operation. Her idea of food preparation was to buy frozen things in bulk, take them out of the freezer the night before to thaw, then come in the next day and warm them up in the oven. When the food landed on the plates, it was tough, slobbery, and nearly inedible.

And my job was to be her assistant! I was not allowed to cook. She had no interest in my advice. The fact that I had run high-class food and beverage operations for a $69 million corporation meant nothing here. Instead, my days were filled with cleaning tables, sweeping floors, and doing dishes—by hand. We had no dishwashing machine.

So this was the American dream? You start as a dishwasher, and twenty-three years later, you get to be . . . a dishwasher.

My frustration grew exponentially, and apparently it showed. My boss complained to Charlie, "This guy you sent me won't do what I say. Honestly, I don't want him anymore. Please give me someone else."

Charlie called us both into his office.

"You are simply not doing your job," she told me right off the bat.

"Oh, really?" I shot back. "It seems to me that you are the one dragging leaves and dirt into the kitchen, making a mess, so that I have to clean up after you when you finally leave."

"No, you are the one who has no eye for details."

> So this was the American dream? You start as a dishwasher, and twenty-three years later, you get to be . . . a dishwasher.

We were about to begin yelling at each other simultaneously when Charlie intervened. "Now just a minute." Turning to the woman, he said, "I've known this man for more than twenty years now. He's a man of character. If you give him a toothbrush and tell him to clean the floor with it, he'll get down on all fours and do it. He sincerely wants to help."

"Really?" the woman said, unconvinced.

"Yes. Now I want you two to go back and find a way to work this out," Charlie said.

I was aghast to show up for work the next day and find that

what Charlie had obviously meant as a metaphor, she was going to take literally! She handed me a toothbrush and said, "Use this to clean the grout between the floor tiles in this kitchen. I want them looking like new."

She couldn't be serious, could she?

Yes, she could. Any chunk of self-pride was shattered in that moment. The conceited restaurant manager of the past was reduced to the level of a galley slave, spending his evening scrubbing away with a toothbrush.

SHOWDOWN WITH GOD

This tension went on for about six months. *How can Charlie, whom I love and respect, let this continue?* I wondered.

I finally came home one day and said to Karen, "I'm going downstairs to the spare bedroom and locking myself in with God. He has to show me what in the world I'm supposed to do here. I will seek the Lord and put everything before him. Don't bring me any food. No visitors, no phone calls, no conversations."

I closed the door behind me that day, slammed the walls with my fist, and started unloading on God. "Why did you bring me here? There are no Muslims, no Arabs, no Jews. Instead, I have to deal with farmers and nut cases. These hillbillies can't do anything right! What's the point?" I started listing all my irritations, the people I couldn't stand, the jobs I hated. I told God I had unplugged myself from all my former contacts and opportunities to come out here and live in the sticks. Now what was he going to do about it?

Sometime as the evening wore on, as I lay with my face on the floor, I fell asleep. I woke up only when the morning light began coming in the window. My rage was spent now. But my outlook was still dismal. "Lord, I want to die," I said in a quiet voice, leaning against the wall. "I don't want to be here. I don't want to deal with this type of Christianity. How about if Karen and I just pack our bags and drive away, never to return?"

The room was silent. I waited to see if God had anything fresh to say. What came into my heart after a few minutes was not a statement but a question.

Do you remember Joshua, who used to be in the boys' program here?

Yes, of course I remembered Joshua. Tough kid from the mean streets of New York. Big-time troublemaker. Always getting the other guys to follow him into mischief. One of our biggest challenges. Yet over time, he had softened his heart and let the Lord overhaul his personality.

What do you think changed Joshua? How did he get to be a young man of integrity? Why is he now leading other young people as a Christian youth worker?

My mind traced back to various conversations and prayer times I'd had with Joshua. I remembered him coming into the kitchen during the afternoons just to talk. A number of the guys in the program did that. They liked to hear my stories of how I grew up. They especially liked the war stories from my time with the PLO. They thought that was cool.

I had unplugged myself from all my former contacts and opportunities to come out here and live in the sticks. Now what was God going to do about it?

I would give them pieces of advice along the way. I'd tell a story and then say something like, "So I guess I learned that day that fighting can produce as many new problems as it solves old ones," or some other lesson. I was touching their young lives, and they listened to me attentively.

Pretty soon I realized that I had been a father figure to guys like Joshua, a signpost pointing them in the right direction. I was also an open ear for them to talk to. God had placed me in their lives for a strategic reason—even as I was mopping the floor and cleaning pans. He had been using me without my recognizing it.

I cried for quite a long time that day. I then got up, unlocked the door, and went to see Charlie. I apologized for my lousy attitude. I admitted I had wanted to leave Heartland but that God had shown me in the spare room how that would be a big mistake.

He got down on his knees with me. We wept and prayed together, thanking God for his mercy and love. It marked a turning point for me. I realized that if I allowed the devil to direct my thoughts, I would end up nowhere. But if I would hold on to the purpose of this place, God would put me to good use.

This was the beginning of a vision for my future. I saw the value of taking care of hurt and needy kids whom nobody else wanted. That vision would expand later to the chaotic refugee camps of the Gaza Strip. But in order for that to happen, I needed to be stripped of my self-centeredness, greed, and self-pity. I needed to learn to keep persevering in hard times. God was looking for humble servants, not egotistical princes. I had to choose which I would be.

AN OLD SCORE TO SETTLE

Sometime in 1998, I received an invitation to a Christian conference for missionaries working in the Muslim nations. It would be held on Cyprus, the island in the eastern Mediterranean about 125 miles off Beirut. They wanted me to speak on the topic of "Love Your Enemies."

I was excited to go, because it would be an opportunity to thank those who were working so faithfully among my people. I wanted to tell them that they were my heroes. I knew I would meet a lot of people with the same passion I carried for sharing Christ in the Muslim world.

One of the conference organizers who had connections in the travel industry said he could get a great price on my ticket. I was glad to accept his offer to help. "What would be the itinerary?" I asked as we were talking.

"We'll get you to Chicago," he explained, "and then you'll fly nonstop on Royal Jordanian Airlines to Amman. From there you transfer for the short hop back to Nicosia, Cyprus."

My heart stopped. "Um, did you say Royal Jordanian?" I finally asked.

"Yes—why?"

"I can't do that. Isn't there some other airline I can take?"

"Well, yes—but not at this great price. What's the problem?"

"I have quite a history with Jordan, going back to my early days," I explained. "When I was with Fatah, we—well, let me just say that we stirred up a lot of dust there. And I happen to know that they haven't forgotten my name."

Just six months before, my father had gone to visit my brother and his family in Amman. Immediately, he was detained at the airport. The Jordanian officials could not charge him directly with any crime, but they insisted that he show up at the police headquarters every morning at eight o'clock for interrogation. They asked a lot of questions about his family. What really caught his attention was when they said mysteriously, "Oh, and what about your son in America? Is he coming back? Maybe he could help you here in this situation."

My father deflected their suggestion, of course. But this little charade went on for nineteen days. My father would arrive every morning at eight, sit in the waiting room for hours, and then be allowed to leave in the afternoon. As the days went by, there was no more questioning—just a lot of sitting around. Finally they told him he didn't need to come anymore.

When I heard about all this in a phone call from my brother, the message to me was ominous: The Jordanians have not forgotten about you. They still remember that you tried to assassinate the crown prince. Your name is still on their list. They would love to get their hands on you once again.

Now I would have to cause extra trouble for the conference organizer who was arranging my ticket by insisting on a different routing, and pay hundreds of dollars more—or else just not go to Cyprus at all. Which should I choose? I talked it over with Karen.

Then the Holy Spirit dropped a question into my mind: Why

not go through Jordan? If I were ever going to have a ministry in the Middle East, I would have to face this sooner or later.

Yes, but . . .

I let the subject rest for a few days. My friend, however, needed to know what I was going to do. The travel agent needed to know whether I was going.

I talked with Karen some more. I also aired it with Charlie. I said I couldn't go on avoiding Jordan for the rest of my life.

Both of them were apprehensive. So was I, to be honest. I kept praying about what to do. I rehearsed what I would say if questioned in Amman. "It is true that a very long time ago, when I was still a teenager, I fought with Fatah in this country. Many things have changed since then. I am now a naturalized American citizen, as you can see by my passport. I have a wife and two grown children back in America. And God has made a great difference in my life over the years. I am truly sorry and repentant for the trouble I caused here back in the 1960s. I ask for your mercy and forgiveness."

> My heart stopped. "Did you say Royal Jordanian?"

Finally, I concluded that I must go to the conference and use Royal Jordanian to get there. I could not retreat. This matter needed to be resolved. I planned the dates to allow some time with family members in both Jordan and Lebanon before going on to Cyprus. "Lord, guide and protect my steps," I prayed.

"TILL DEATH DO US PART"

But before I left, I wanted to take care of two things. Both had to do with my family relationships.

First, I wanted to publicly affirm my love for Karen in a *church* wedding ceremony, giving her the diamond ring I hadn't been able to afford that day long ago when we'd stood up before the justice of the peace. I planned it as a surprise with Charlie, who was serving as the Heartland pastor, having been in the ministry as a young man before entering the business world.

I even went out and bought a special dress for Karen to wear. I arranged for Ben and Farah to come from Kansas City, along with all of Karen's family. They only said to her that they missed us and wanted to come visit for a weekend reunion of sorts.

At the end of the service that morning, Charlie said to the audience of about 350, "Now before we leave today, I want to ask Karen and Tass to step forward, please. Something wonderful is going to take place." At this, Karen's sister appeared with a bridal bouquet, our son stepped forward with the diamond in his pocket, and our daughter came up as well with my wedding ring. Karen was absolutely speechless.

"These two special people," Charlie explained, "were married back in 1974 in a civil ceremony. Today we will celebrate with them a fully Christian marriage in a church. Dearly beloved, we are gathered today in the sight of God and these witnesses . . ." And off he went into the familiar ceremony.

I was smiling, of course. Karen got weak in the knees. When the diamond ring came out, she nearly fainted. There were tears of joy all over the sanctuary that day. Before God, we affirmed our vows to love, honor, and cherish each other "till death do us part." In the back of our minds, of course, we hoped that the day of deaths would not come anytime soon. We fervently prayed that God would allow us to serve him side by side for many more years.

The other family matter I needed to attend to was to come clean with Ben, now twenty-four years old, about the fact that I was not his biological father. We had never talked about this in our family. I had adopted him and given him the family name Saada long ago, when he was too young to remember. Now I wanted him to know the truth and how much I loved him, regardless.

So I asked him to step into my office. I worried about how he would react. Would this news unnerve him? Would he be upset that he hadn't known earlier? I prayed for God to give me the right words and the right tone.

"My son, let me tell you something important," I began nervously. "Since it's not certain whether I'll return from Jordan, I need to sort this out before I go."

"What's going on?" he asked, a puzzled look on his face.

I took a deep breath and exhaled. I felt the pressure rising within me. Finally, I came forward with the words: "You know, when I first met your mother, you were already six weeks old. Therefore you are not actually of my blood. But I've always loved you like my own son. I have never seen you as anything else. The Lord has put you deep into my heart. You will always be very special to me."

There, it was finally out.

Ben did not look shocked at all. "Oh, yes, I already knew that!" he said. "I didn't bring it up to you because I didn't think it was very important."

I was shocked.

"How did you know?" I asked.

"Grandma gave it away by accident a couple of years ago. We were out at her lake house and talking about how Seth"—a cousin—"was adopted. I said something like, 'I wonder how he feels about that.'

> We affirmed our vows before God that we would love, honor, and cherish each other "till death do us part."

"And Grandma said, 'Well, how does it feel for you? You're totally integrated into the family.'

"I looked at her like, *What are you talking about?* And then she got this embarrassed expression on her face. She knew she had spilled the beans."

This led to a wonderful exchange between Ben and me that day. He told how he had talked with his pastor about being an adopted child. The pastor had wisely said, "Did your father ever treat you like you were not his?"

"No," Ben had answered.

"Did he ever treat you differently from your sister?"

Again: "No."

"Then I'd say to let the matter rest. This man entered your life at an early stage and took good care of you. Give God thanks for that, and go on from here."

Whew! What a relief!

Now if only the talks with the Jordanian authorities would go so smoothly.

CHAPTER 13

LIVING ON THE EDGE

I TRIED TO STAY STRONG THAT DAY at the Kansas City airport as I said good-bye to my family, but it was extremely difficult. Farah was crying hard, and Karen and Ben were close to tears. "It will be all right," I said. "The Lord will go ahead of me." But on the inside, I wasn't as confident as I acted.

I went through security and took my seat in the boarding area. Looking through the glass, I saw my family still standing there, watching me. Was this really what I should be doing? I almost bolted for the exit right up until the flight was called.

I got as far as Chicago. Then, as I tightened my seat belt on the Royal Jordanian jet that day, I couldn't help wondering if this was an omen of things to come. At the other end of this flight, would I be tightened and strapped down for the rest of my life? Would this be my last day as a free man? It was possible, I knew—but God had nudged me to make this trip, and he had my best interests at heart.

Twelve hours later, we landed at the airport I had not seen since my forced departure from Fatah more than twenty-five years before. How good it felt to be back in the Middle East again, reading

Arabic signs and seeing crowds of people who looked like me! As I walked down the concourse, my thoughts quickly turned, however, to getting ready for passport control. Was I prepared for all the questions that would soon come my way?

Would this be my last day as a free man?

I waited in line until my turn came to approach the agent. He was dressed in a crisp uniform, and he wore sunglasses, which meant I couldn't read his eyes. I slid my American passport across the counter, then held my breath.

He opened my document, looked at my photo there, and studied my information. He typed something into his computer, then stared at his screen. I thought the seconds would never pass.

Finally he looked up at me. "Your name?"

"Taysir Saada," I answered, trying to keep my voice on an even level.

"And the name of your grandfather?"

I gave him that information as well.

"What passport did you have before this one?" he then asked.

Uh-oh; that's it, I said to myself. *Now he's onto my trail. Here comes the crackdown.*

I was just ready to answer, "A Jordanian one, sir . . ." when suddenly I saw the corners of his mouth turn up in a smile. He didn't wait for my reply. Instead, he handed the passport to his assistant and said, "Stamp it!"

With the stamp of approval applied, I received the passport back into my hands. "Go on ahead. Have a good time in Jordan!" the agent said with a laugh.

I could not explain what had just happened. He had started to cross-examine me, but then he stopped for some reason. I had passed the first gauntlet.

Now what would happen at baggage claim? Would someone pull me aside there? After all, I wasn't by any means out of the airport yet. Was anybody following me? I glanced over my shoulder to check. No, at least not for now.

My luggage was waiting on the carousel. At this point, another worry hit my brain: *What will the customs people think of the Christian literature I'm carrying? They'll know I have an Islamic name. Will they conclude that I'm a convert? If so, I'll be in a different kind of trouble.* This was a country where pastors had been deported and evangelical churches shut down more than once.

As I pulled my suitcases away from the rest, I saw a muscular man near the exit. He, too, wore sunglasses. Suddenly he called out in English, "Over here! Come over here!"

Did he mean *me*?

Yes, apparently so. Motioning to me, he repeated his instruction, "Come on over here—with your luggage!" When I got closer, he said, "Here, let me help you."

I told myself he could be just a normal porter with good English skills. On the other hand, he could also be a "plant" by the security forces to entrap me.

"Follow me," he instructed, picking up one of my cases. He headed out the terminal door toward the taxi area, avoiding the customs checkpoint altogether. There he put one suitcase in the nearest trunk. The taxi driver loaded the other one. I was busy looking around for anything or anybody who appeared suspicious. I told myself this taxi guy could also be part of the capture team. *Well, couldn't he?*

I turned once again to say thank you to the man in the sunglasses. He had vanished. I couldn't see him anywhere. Had he been just a normal porter—or a "special messenger" from above? I will never know.

I got into the cab. I checked to see if the rear doors had handles on the inside for getting out. Yes, they did.

"Where do you want to go?" the driver asked me in Arabic.

If he was intent on taking me off to some secret interrogation center, he didn't act like it. I pulled out my little address book and gave him a street and number where my cousin lived. He nodded, set his meter, and headed out into the traffic. He seemed relaxed as he drove.

I still kept watching him every minute. I looked around the taxi for signs of a weapon. I could find none.

Finally, he pulled up to the address I had given him. He got out of the cab to remove my luggage. I paid the fare—and he drove away. Nothing had happened! There I stood, in the middle of a street in Amman, still as free as when I had left the United States the day before.

DISCOVERED

I hadn't told this cousin I was coming because I didn't know how my trip would unfold once I landed. Now I walked up to the door and knocked. I waited.

"Who's there?" a female voice asked from the other side.

"It's me, Taysir Saada," I said, and then gave my father's name. "Is this the house of my cousin Ahmed?"*

"One moment," the woman's voice replied. I kept listening. I could hear her talking about me to someone in the house.

Then the door flew open. "Taysir! My cousin!" Ahmed greeted me with a warm hug. "Welcome, step inside!"

I entered with my luggage and forgot, at least for the time being, about security risks. We sat down together in his pleasantly furnished living room. We began recounting stories of days gone by, of growing up in Qatar, and asking one another what was happening with this relative and that one. Everything was comfortable. His wife served us tea. We kept talking for maybe half an hour.

At the same time, he was absentmindedly flipping through TV channels with his remote control. He happened to land on the Christian interview program *The 700 Club*, dubbed into Arabic. He kept going up the range, then came back again.

Looking at me, he said, "You know, I saw this program one time when they had a segment on training Fatah fighters. They interviewed this one guy who was formerly with Fatah. They didn't use his real name, but . . . was that *you*, by any chance?"

*Pseudonym

A few years before, I had indeed been interviewed by *The 700 Club*. So I told my cousin the truth. "Yes, it was me."

He laughed and said, "So I figured you out! It was very interesting. I watched the whole thing. This fellow on the program, this former Fatah fighter, had become a Christian, they said. Does that mean that *you* have become a Christian, Taysir?" He was staring intently at me as he spoke.

"Yes, that is correct," I replied.

His wife immediately got up and left the room, taking their young son with her. My cousin's attitude turned noticeably more cool. "I see," he responded, and then fell silent.

> His wife immediately got up and left the room, taking their young son with her.

The easy banter of conversation we had enjoyed up to this point was now gone. I tried to talk about a couple of other topics, but his answers were short and to the point. I was getting the message that I was no longer welcome here.

"I think it would be good for me to find a hotel now," I said. "Or perhaps I could use your phone to call my brother." He lived there in Amman, too. Fourteen years younger than me, he looked up to me and wasn't likely to do me harm.

Ahmed was willing to let me use his phone. Soon I was on my way to my brother's house. The reception there was cordial—although by the next day, I could sense a change. It became apparent that my brother and my cousin had talked. Meanwhile, my sister-in-law disappeared, going to stay with her parents. I never saw her again.

When my brother asked me if it was true that I had become a Christian, I, of course, said yes. I could tell he was curious about this. "So what happened?" he asked. That opened the door for me to give my full story.

My brother had many questions, and we spent hours talking about them. He also wanted to know all about life in America because he wasn't very happy in Jordan. We started talking about the idea that he might emigrate. He was very interested in that possibility.

All during the week, I worried about whether he or my cousin might call the authorities. Neither of them did. We had a nice visit, and when it was time to board the plane for the rest of my itinerary, everything went smoothly. The Lord had guided my steps and overseen my plans so that I would be free to come here again in the future. He had known all along that I'd be safe—or else he "erased" my name from any Jordanian records that might have incriminated me.

I had trusted my inner impression to go this route as something that God was speaking to me. I had walked ahead in faith. Now I could only give God thanks for his protection.

APOLOGY ACCEPTED

At the mission conference in Cyprus, I met Christian leaders and workers from many countries. On the day I was invited to speak, I gave my testimony. I told about my past as a refugee child, about running away from home at age seventeen to join Fatah, about becoming a sniper, and then the unusual circumstances by which I had gone to America. I told about my remarkable conversion in Charlie Sharpe's living room. I expressed my desire for my Palestinian people to know and trust Jesus.

In the middle of speaking, however, I began to sense tension in the room among the Arab pastors. While the Western missionaries were relaxed and interested in what I was saying, I could tell that the Arabs did not appreciate it. I couldn't just ignore this undercurrent.

So I interrupted my testimony. "I need to stop here and say something important," I said. "Pastors, elders, missionaries—I feel an impression to ask your forgiveness for the terrible things that have been done to you by us Muslims. I admit to you that in my early days, I myself made life very difficult for Christians in Amman. I am very sorry for what I did.

"You have prepared the ground for the message of Christ. I am here today only because people like you found the truth of Jesus and then shared it with me. I appreciate you so much. Thank you, thank you for your ministry over the years. I am so sorry for making things difficult for you. Please forgive us. Please don't ever give up this work! Many of us Muslims are going to respond to the call of Christ in the days and years ahead."

By now I was weeping as I spoke. It was a breakthrough moment. I saw heads nodding all over the room. I then proceeded to finish my remarks on what God had done in my life. People came to me afterward to thank me for my apology and to express their love and forgiveness.

I met many important contacts at this event that would prove to be strategic in the years ahead. One was a Swiss man named Linus, who headed up HMK*, an organization that seeks to serve the persecuted church. It was inspired originally by a Romanian pastor of Jewish descent, Richard Wurmbrand, who also began Voice of the Martyrs in the United States.

> "I am here today only because people like you found the truth of Jesus and then shared it with me."

Linus later e-mailed me about a Moroccan who was in trouble because of his Christian faith. "Can you get him a visa somehow to enter America?" Linus wanted to know. I said I would try.

This contact opened up doors for me in Switzerland, Germany, France, and England, countries to which so many Middle Eastern Muslims have migrated. Still to this day, I go back to speak to groups that have been organized by HMK.

Apparently, God really did intend for me to attend the Cyprus conference.

A VERY STRANGE "MOVIE"

Sometime after returning to Heartland, I was sitting in the dining hall one December day reading my Bible when a most unusual

---

*Hilfe für Mensch und Kirche

thing happened. It would end up defining the next season of ministry in my life.

My eyes were open as I sat there, but instead of tables and benches, I saw myself at the wheel of a white Mercury Villager van on a seemingly endless road. In the passenger seat was a younger man. His head was turned so I couldn't make out his face, but I saw he was wearing a Jewish *yarmulke* on his head. How strange—especially for someone like me.

Behind us, the middle seat had been removed. Our luggage was there, rather than being stored in the far back of the vehicle, as usual.

On both sides of the road before us were mosques, synagogues, and churches. As the "movie" played, I saw the two of us getting out of the van and going into a church. I walked to the front and started cautioning the audience about the dangers of Islam. I told them it would try to sweep over the whole world, including America.

Next I saw us going into a synagogue. There I confessed to them what I had done as a Fatah fighter and asked their forgiveness.

Next we went into a mosque. I told them what God had done in my life, how he had radically changed me from a hateful person into someone full of love.

And then the "movie" stopped.

I did not immediately draw any conclusions from this experience. It was pretty bizarre, and I just let the matter rest.

Two weeks later, I was in the midst of looking for a van for our restaurant manager at Heartland, who needed one for transporting supplies. I called a Quincy dealer and described what I was looking for. He said he had a good possibility on the lot, so I sent one of our staff members to bring it out.

A few hours later, I came out of my office and saw that he had returned—but not with the van I had discussed. Instead, here was a white van *exactly* like the one in my vision.

"What's this?" I said to him. "This isn't the van I talked to the salesman about."

"Yes, I know," he answered. "But on the way, I saw this one for sale at another dealer. And it was such a good deal—a better value for the price than what you had arranged. So I bought it for you instead." I was a little perturbed, until he told me the price. I had to admit he had found a real bargain.

Then I looked inside the van.

The middle seat was missing.

Immediately I was perplexed. Had God been trying to tell me something back in the dining room? Apparently so. I went to see Charlie. I told him the whole story. I said the van I had seen was now sitting outside.

> I saw myself at the wheel of a white Mercury Villager van on a seemingly endless road.

"Do you think God is asking me to go out on the road and talk to people about him?" I said.

"I don't know," he replied. "Let's pray about it for a few days."

A week later, we talked again. "Have you received any kind of directive in your prayer time?" I asked him.

"Neither yes nor no, Tass," he said. "So my advice is, go ahead and get started. Let's both ask the Lord to stop you if this is not his idea. Otherwise, pursue the vision."

I liked that response.

When I began to talk it all through with Karen, however, I could read the concern in her eyes. The thought of me leaving for an extended period of time brought back bad memories of my California time years before. She did not make a direct comparison, but I could tell she was not thrilled with the prospect.

We prayed together on a number of occasions about whether this was really the Lord's will for me to do. We fasted. We talked and talked. Eventually, we came to an agreement.

I began collecting an air mattress, a sleeping bag, and other supplies for my van. In one sense, the whole thing was crazy. I didn't have any appointments or speaking engagements set up. I didn't have a booking agency to call ahead on my behalf. I would be heading out into the void.

But then I remembered how Jesus had sent his twelve disciples out under similar conditions. His instructions were awfully minimal. The main thing he had said was, "Go . . . to the lost sheep of Israel. As you go, preach this message: 'The kingdom of heaven is near.'"* He told them not even to take a supply of money, but just to walk from town to town and see what would happen.

They went—and experienced incredible miracles. Would God do the same for me on the open road? I certainly hoped so.

When Charlie asked how much money I was thinking of taking along, I said, "None at all. God has impressed me not to take any, and not to plan a route. I'm supposed to go just where he leads me."

"Are you sure you heard it like that?" he asked.

"Yes, absolutely."

CHASED OUT

I set a departure date of February 7, 2001—a Wednesday. A day or two before, some good friends of ours came to say good-bye. The woman was an elementary school teacher, and she gave me an envelope. "Don't open this until the twelfth of the month," she instructed, saying nothing more.

"Okay," I replied. I assumed it was artwork from some of her students.

As we looked into each other's eyes that morning, Karen and I became emotional. Neither one of us could come up with the right words, it seemed. We both knew I could face danger by heading into mosques with my message. We hugged one another and kissed, crying all the time. We said a final prayer, and then I headed west.

That weekend I stopped at some Kansas City churches and also a synagogue, as I felt I had been instructed to do. I didn't knock at every door I passed, of course. I tried to discern God's direction for where I should stop.

The response was disappointing. Nobody quite knew what to do with me. They would politely listen for a short while and then find a way to get on with the rest of their schedule. I certainly was not invited to make any public addresses.

*Matthew 10:6-7

The only encouragement I received was the next Monday, when I opened the envelope from the school teacher. The contents were not pictures or poems, after all. Inside was more than four hundred dollars! I thanked the Lord for this surprise and kept driving west.

My stops in Colorado Springs and Denver didn't go any better than in Kansas City. I went to Friday prayers at one Denver mosque. After the meeting, I sat talking with the imam and other worshipers around me. "Does the Qur'an say anything about Ishmael and Hagar?" I asked.

"Very little," the imam answered. "There is, however, another set of writings called *The Beginning and the End* that has some stories about them."

"That's interesting. Did you know that a lot is written about them in the Bible?" I asked. "We Arabs are the sons of Ishmael, and it tells all about him in the first part, called Genesis."

"Oh, really?" they said.

"Yes. Abraham was his father, and Hagar was his mother. . . ." I went on to describe the blessings that had been pronounced upon Ishmael, our ancestor.

Soon the imam spoke up. "Wait a minute," he said. "Are you Muslim or Christian?"

"I was a Muslim," I admitted. "Then I became a Christian."

Immediately he began yelling at me. "How can you take the liberty to come in here and defile our holy ground in this mosque? You are a heathen! An infidel! Get out!"

I looked around the circle of those who had been listening to me. One man with sharp-looking eyes who had been smiling at me as I spoke now gave a subtle tilt of his head, as if to say, *You'd better run, quickly.*

I jumped up and headed for the exit. The crowd followed me. Everybody was shouting at once. In the midst of the uproar, I heard close behind me the voice of the man who had signaled me. "Psst! Got a business card? Throw it down!"

I reached into my pocket, still running hard, and pulled out my business card. I dropped it on the sidewalk without missing a step. Like a flash I was into my van and zooming down the street. I had escaped!

A few hours later, my cell phone rang. It was the man with the smile. "I'm a convert, too—but I stay in the mosque to try to influence others," he said. "Tass, you're awfully courageous. They could have killed you, you know."

"Yes, I suppose you're right," I said. "But I believe this is something God wants me to do anyway." I had the privilege of encouraging him over lunch before I left town. I was able to give him some outreach materials and to pray with him.

WANDERING BEDOUIN

I drove north on Interstate 25 across the snowy plateaus of Wyoming. When I got to the junction with Interstate 90, I seriously considered heading back east. After all, weren't there a lot more Arabs and Jews in places like Detroit and New York?

I called Karen. We prayed together on the phone. In the end, we agreed together that I should keep heading west toward Seattle.

I realize this sounds like I was just wandering aimlessly, like a Bedouin in the desert. My trip certainly did not resemble an orderly "speaking tour." But somehow, I sensed I was doing what God had instructed me to do. If nothing else, I was learning to trust him for my daily needs. And I was finding ways to express his truth better to all kinds of people.

I stopped to see a Lebanese friend named Bill who lived just east of Seattle. He welcomed me warmly and invited me to stay at his house for several days while we visited various houses of worship. Once again, church people were skeptical of my warnings about Islam. An Orthodox rabbi with a long, beautiful beard was hospitable and spent a long time talking with me—until he got worried that I would try to convert his people. "I don't convert Jewish people," I tried to assure him. "I only pray that they may find their Messiah."

He laughed and shook his head. "Just be careful," he admonished. When I showed up the next morning at seven o'clock for his regularly scheduled prayer service, the door was tightly locked. Nobody would answer my knocking or even phoning.

Altogether, in Seattle I visited half a dozen synagogues and eleven mosques, with Bill's help. One imam listened respectfully to my testimony. When I finished, he had tears in his eyes. "That is an amazing story," he said. "I've never heard something like that. You have been touched by an angel. There is power coming from your words."

I was surprised. "Are you a Christian, too?" I asked him.

"No. But I understand what you're telling me. We live in a remarkable time; things happen, and we don't know why. May God bless you and lead you in his ways."

We exchanged phone numbers and talked casually several times later. For some reason he didn't want to talk about faith issues on the phone, however. So I invited him for coffee. He was reluctant. "I can't talk to you anymore," he said. "I need some distance from all this. I have obligations that will have me traveling soon, both here in the United States and also in Syria."

"Would you like to meet me at the mosque?" I offered.

"It is Allah's house. You can come whenever you like—as long as you do not speak with me there. Others have noticed you stopping at my office after Friday prayers, and they are beginning to ask questions."

I could do nothing more but pray for this earnest and sincere man.

LOVE FOR AN "ENEMY"

During my time in Seattle, a friend phoned from Los Angeles, inviting me to an annual conference of Christian Arabs and Messianic Jews. Some four hundred people would be there, he said. He wanted me to speak briefly. It was a very long way to drive. But I felt the Holy Spirit wanted me to go. So I did.

It turned out to be an amazing boost to my spirits. Every presentation was so inspiring. Just ahead of the time I was to speak, they introduced a young Israeli named Schmuel.* When he came to the podium, my jaw dropped in shock. Even though I had not seen his face before, I recognized him as exactly the young man in the yarmulke I had seen in my vision! I could hardly believe it.

He told about growing up on an Israeli kibbutz and, after some early teenage rebellion, being drafted into the army. While there, several of his closest friends were among twenty-two soldiers killed in one blast by a Palestinian suicide bomber. He began to hate Arabs intensely. After leaving the service, he fell into a severe depression fueled by alcoholism. To get away from all the ugliness in his life, he had escaped to Los Angeles.

> I recognized him as exactly the young man in the yarmulke I had seen in my vision! I could hardly believe it.

A friend invited him to church in 1998. He went and was agitated as he sat through the service. But he felt the love of the congregation and was impressed by their love for Israel. When challenged to read the Bible, he did so. There he found evidence of God's love and faithfulness to the people of Israel, even when they sinned against him. He also found that the Messiah had indeed come to save him.

When he finished speaking to the audience, I rushed to the front to stretch out my hand. "Schmuel, my name is Tass," I said. "I am a former Fatah fighter—"

The young man instantly pulled back his hand and stared at me.

Before he could say a word, I continued, "My friend, I want you to know that because of the Messiah, I love you." He relaxed slightly.

He was considerably younger than I was, so we would not have been combatants at the same time. Nevertheless, we both knew what it was to carry and fire a deadly weapon in the service of our cause. Had we faced one another on a battlefield or in a narrow street in the past, one of us—or perhaps both—would certainly have died on the spot.

*Pseudonym

Just at that moment, the moderator of the meeting called everyone to form small prayer circles. I found myself with Schmuel, two Jordanians, and a Jewish rabbi. God came down into the circle that day. I prayed with tears for the peace of Jerusalem. I prayed for peace between our peoples. The others prayed fervently as well for God's Kingdom to come and his will to be done on earth, as it is in heaven. What an incredible experience!

When at last I was introduced to speak to the group, the first thing I did was call Schmuel up to the front beside me. I looked him in the eye and asked his forgiveness. "I am truly sorry for the loss of your friends that day," I said. "And I am sorry for all the attacks and murders my people have done to yours."

He was a little unsure how to respond. We stood there trying to read one another. Finally he said, "If you will forgive me, I will forgive you as well." We then hugged each other.

I then began to address the crowd. I asked all the Jews present to forgive me. I asked the Christian Arabs to forgive me as well for the pressure I had created upon them. The crowd became emotional. The presence of the Holy Spirit that day was apparent across the room.

After the conference, I told Schmuel about my vision. I described the Jewish person I had seen in the minivan. I asked him if he would consider helping me bring Jews and Palestinians together. He assured me he would pray about such a joint ministry.

When we then went for a bite of lunch, we had falafel sandwiches. They were a bit dry, and I noticed Schmuel having trouble swallowing. So I went to get him a glass of water.

When I handed it to him, he smiled and said, "No, first *you* drink! I need to see how it affects you."

"Oh, yes!" I said with a laugh as I took a sip. "You want to be sure the water is safe, right? Old habits die hard."

We enjoyed the little joke, and our bond to one another was strengthened even more. This would be the beginning of a close friendship.

TURNING POINT

From time to time, I would leave the road to go back to Missouri and be with my wife for a while. Then I would strike out again on the mission I felt God had given me, to warn the churches of the dangers of aggressive Islam.

Early in my travels, I stopped at one church in Kirkland, Washington. I asked the woman at the reception desk if I might see the pastor. I told her I was a Palestinian, a former Muslim who now followed Christ.

Within minutes the man came to his office door to welcome me with outstretched arms. I looked at him and was surprised to see that his eyes seemed wet and reddened. "Welcome, friend," he said. "You're surprised that I've been crying?"

"I am, indeed."

"You know, for a week now I've been praying that God would send me someone like you. And here you are—out of thin air!"

"For a week?"

"Yes, because our city has so many Muslims. I want to do something; I want to learn how to work among them. These people are very important to me. I've been praying that someone would come and teach me how to go forward."

I stood amazed at how the Holy Spirit had opened this opportunity.

"How long are you free?" he asked.

"As long as you like," I answered.

"All right. I want you to speak to my congregation for a whole week, every night. On Saturday and Sunday we will organize a big conference."

He began advertising in newspapers and on the radio, so that crowds came from everywhere. I told my story and emphasized how important it was for Christian people to care about Muslim work. I thanked the pastor for standing up for this vital area of ministry.

But this seemed to be the exception rather than the rule. Most churches remained apathetic to my message—until September 11.

All of a sudden, interest in the Muslim question shot upward. Pastors and congregations wanted to know who had attacked this nation, what motivated them, who else might be planning future attacks, and what could be done to prevent this from happening. "What does the word *jihad* mean?" they asked. "Why are Muslims so mad at us?"

I tried to emphasize that while we hate the sin of terrorism, we must still love the sinners who are trapped in it. "Many Muslims in America right now are almost afraid to come out of their homes," I said. "You can put your faith into action by helping them through this hard time. Go with them to the store, or take their grocery list and go shopping for them. They need to see the reality of Jesus' words that we love our enemies and pray for those who persecute us."

In February 2002, I was invited by an Arab pastor in San Francisco to speak in his church about outreach. That was my only opportunity in that area; I became very discouraged, with my money supply almost exhausted. I was skipping meals and even hitchhiking because I couldn't afford gasoline.

Most churches remained apathetic to my message—until September 11.

After fasting for twelve days, I was desperate. "God, have I made a mistake?" I prayed. "Nothing is opening up for me here. I can't even afford to get back home now. What is going to become of me?" I knelt in prayer that evening so long that I fell asleep and didn't wake up until the next morning, when the phone jarred me.

It was a pastor inviting me to speak to a ministerial lunch meeting that very day! At that event, invitations came quickly, from all corners of the room. "Help my church understand Islam better," the pastors said. "We really need your message. We'll be glad to take care of your expenses while you are with us." All of a sudden, my distress was turned around. The Lord wanted me there after all.

These contacts, on the West Coast and elsewhere, became the constituency that enabled my wife and me to start a nonprofit organization called "Hope for Ishmael," whose mission is to serve Arabs and Jews by reconciling them to the Father and then to one another. We began dreaming of what could be done in the Gaza Strip and the West Bank for children, for their parents, and for all who yearn for peace in the midst of strife and death. We would be a voice for reconciliation and hope.

CHAPTER 14

ARAFAT
ONCE
MORE

THERE WAS ONE OTHER MIDDLE EASTERN COUNTRY that might have an old score to settle with me, I realized. That would be Israel. After all, I had caused a lot of damage there back in my Fatah days. But did they know for sure it was *me*? Out of the thousands of Fatah fighters, would they have tracked my name?

A pastor in the suburb of Grandview, Missouri, south of Kansas City, invited me to speak in his church. Following that meeting, he told me that he would soon be leading a Holy Land tour for his people, and he wanted my wife and me to go along, at his expense. We gratefully accepted.

When we landed at Ben Gurion Airport outside Tel Aviv, an odd sensation swept over me. Here was a thriving country that I had once wanted to wipe off the map. Now I felt almost as if I were coming home! Why was that? Because this was a nation of people whom God loved, and whom I now loved too.

At passport control, no questions were raised about me. As far as the Israelis were concerned, I was just another American tourist among more than a million who come every year, fueling Israel's all-important tourism industry. We had a wonderful excursion around the country, seeing the biblical sites and reading the Scriptures that described what had occurred at each place.

The first time I spotted an Israeli soldier, however, I was surprised by the surge of emotion that welled up inside me. Instantly I thought, *How many Palestinians has he killed?* My days of fighting with Fatah suddenly seemed as close as yesterday.

Then I came back to my senses. Quickly I prayed, "Oh, God, where did this come from? Forgive me for assuming the worst about this young guy I don't even know."

I walked in the soldier's direction and said to him, "Excuse me, but I was just wondering—may I pray for you?"

He apparently was accustomed to tourists coming up and asking odd questions. "Yes, it's okay," he said calmly.

So right there on the street, I asked God to bless him, to protect him, and to make himself real to this young man. As I did, I felt the return of God's peace in my own soul.

One day while on the tour bus, I got up the nerve to ask our guide a couple of questions.

"Say, would it be possible to visit Ramallah?" This was the West Bank city just six miles north of Jerusalem where Yasser Arafat's headquarters was.

"No, that's not a good idea for tour groups," she politely replied.

"So then you probably would say the same about visiting the Gaza Strip?" I asked.

She shook her head even more vigorously. *So near, and yet so far,* I thought. *Maybe some other time, under different circumstances.*

The following February (2004), Schmuel and I were able to attend the National Prayer Breakfast in Washington, DC. President George W. Bush was there, of course, with many other dignitaries. During the meal, someone came to ask us if we would be interested in joining a small meeting afterward for those interested in Middle East peace issues. Yes, of course we would!

The moment I walked into the hotel suite that day, I saw Omri Sharon, son of Israeli war hero and then–Prime Minister Ariel Sharon. I recognized him immediately from the many pictures I had seen of him. While waiting for official introductions to get underway, I walked up to him and said, "Omri, do you know what your name means in Arabic?"

He smiled. Then he answered in Arabic, "Yes, of course! It means 'my life.'"

"Oh, you speak Arabic?" I questioned.

"Sure! It's my second language."

"That's wonderful," I said as I shook his hand. "Omri, I'm a Palestinian," I continued, "and in fact I used to be a Fatah fighter."

He tensed up at this and pulled back his hand, but I held onto it. Out of the corner of my eye, I saw his bodyguards reaching under their vests for their revolvers.

"Calm down, boys! Relax!" I said to them. "We're here to talk about peace, remember? By the way, how did you get in here with weapons?"

Omri laughed now and said to his guards, "It's all right; let him be."

> Here was a thriving country that I had once wanted to wipe off the map. Now I felt almost as if I were coming home.

"Omri, I have a message for the prime minister," I then said.

"Yes?"

"When you get home, tell him there's a Palestinian who loves him with all his heart and prays for him every day."

"You're serious?" he asked me, his eyebrows raised.

"Absolutely. It's true."

"Okay," he responded. "I'll tell him. Give me your card."

I gave him one, and he requested a second one for his father. Then he offered, "If you come to Israel, let me know. I'll set up an appointment for you to see the prime minister."

Just then, the leader of the Palestinian delegation joined us. He had heard the last part of the conversation, so he added, "And while you're there, call me as well, so you can visit with Yasser Arafat!"

He had no idea how well I already knew the man—or how badly I would love to see him once more.

BITTERSWEET REUNION

Three months later, in May 2004, I embarked on a journey with several stops. First I went to Jordan, traveling south all the way to the Red Sea port of Aqaba, where I spoke at a reconciliation conference. After crossing over into Egypt and then returning, I finally entered Israel for the meetings that had been promised back in Washington.

I intentionally arrived early in Ramallah so I could get a feel for the city. What I saw was basically twenty-five thousand people living in chaos. Roads were full of potholes, buildings had bullet holes everywhere, and tension seemed to line every face. I saw long lines at the checkpoint between this city and Jerusalem, chewing up hour upon hour of people's time.

I deliberately got into a number of different taxis, just to talk with the drivers. I've found this is a great way to take the pulse of a city. "So what's it like here these days?" I would innocently ask.

"Not good," they said almost universally. "Life is pretty miserable. Ever since the PA* took over, it's actually gotten harder," they claimed. "Abu Ammar himself is great, a real fighter to the end. We love him. But his lieutenants—they don't know how to run things at all. They keep hitting up everybody for bribe money—it's a mess.

"And of course, the Israelis at the border don't trust the PA either, so they crack down all the harder—more rules, more paperwork, more restrictions. It was actually better when they were here running the show! That's a terrible thing to say, I admit, but it's true."

It made me sad to hear these comments. I made mental notes of what I wanted to talk about with my onetime hero. Surely he could get his administration to do better than this.

It was 9:30 at night when two senior officials came to pick me up for my appointment. "We are so happy you have come to visit," they said. "The president will be glad to see you again." I didn't know these two men, but they seemed to have been informed about me.

When we arrived at the headquarters building, I was taken aback

*Palestinian Authority

by the devastation. I knew the Israelis had bombed this place, but I wasn't expecting so much debris and ruin. I stepped inside to the reception area. It was sad, almost desolate. A number of people were just sitting around or even lying on the floor, sleeping—and they appeared to be Europeans or Americans, not Arabs. *What were they doing here?*

When I asked my hosts about this as we walked, they explained, "These are human shields. They have volunteered to stay here in order to dissuade the Israelis from attacking the president again." Well, that was one way for Arafat, the old fox, to keep staying alive.

The farther into the building we got, the more I shook my head. The world-famous Palestinian leader, cowinner of the Nobel Peace Prize back in 1994, was now governing from a dump. I remembered how he used to inspire us in the early days in hunting down the Jews. He was a master strategist. Now the hunter had become the hunted. I felt sorry for him.

We ascended a shabby flight of stairs to the second floor. Nothing was clean; nothing was in order. And then the door to his dusty little office opened.

I walked through the doorway and saw my hero once again. Now seventy-four years old, he looked thoroughly worn out. His lips trembled much more than I ever remembered in the past. Still, he jumped up from his desk and said, "Welcome, welcome, my young comrade! It has been so long since we last saw each other." He came around to greet me with a hug and the traditional kiss on the cheek. He kept holding onto my hand, a very Arab thing to do when meeting an old friend.

"Abu Ammar, it is so good to see you again!" I exclaimed. Then I remembered that the correct title now was "Mr. President." I reminded myself to be more careful from then on.

"Come sit beside me!" he instructed, pulling up a large chair alongside his, behind his desk. I was surprised. He pulled me even closer after I sat down.

"Mr. President, it has been thirty-two years since we last met," I began.

"No, thirty-*four* years," he corrected me.

"Thirty-four?"

"Yes. Just count them. We last saw each other in 1970, at the time of Black September," he insisted. And his math was correct.

Soon he was telling me all that he was doing to help Christian communities in the Palestinian areas. "I'm allowing Christian books and other materials to come in. I want the Christians among us to freely practice their faith. You know, some of the other Palestinian organizations make it hard on Christians in their ranks, but not me. I am their friend!"

I thought to myself, *Boy, his staff has really done their homework on me. They have briefed him not only on my dates of service in Fatah long ago but also on my speaking engagements more recently. He's trying to impress me now. . . .*

"Oh, that's wonderful, Mr. President," I replied. I played along with him, thanking him for his generous spirit. Inside I was praying silently that I could make the most of this appointment, which I had been told would last only fifteen minutes. I was about to jump headlong into talking about Jesus, but the Holy Spirit reined me in. *Relax, Tass—not too fast.*

So we spoke about the old days. We recalled the victory at al-Karameh. I also admitted that I had made some dumb mistakes along the way. "Do you remember my escapades, Mr. President?" I asked.

"Of course, I do! You were one of my worst men. You were ruthless and mean. A lot of the others followed your example, and it cost us much good will in Jordan."

I didn't disagree. "You know, you're right," I said. "I feel very badly about it now. . . . But why did the same mistakes get repeated when you all moved to Lebanon, I wonder? It seemed like not much was learned from what happened in Jordan."

"Oh, in Lebanon the circumstances were entirely different!" he insisted. "Do you know how the Israelis treat the churches?" he asked—obviously changing the subject to something he preferred to talk about. He began pulling pictures out of his desk that showed bombed-out churches, a statue of the Virgin Mary with her head blown off, and other demolitions. "This is what the Israelis do to sacred places of worship!" He rambled on, conveniently forgetting to mention that it was Fatah fighters who had first barricaded themselves inside those churches, inviting Israeli counterattack. The old maestro never missed a chance to make political points against his adversaries.

> I was about to jump headlong into talking about Jesus, but the Holy Spirit reined me in.

I just listened. Occasionally I would chime in with a yes or aha at fitting moments.

TO THE POINT

Finally, I decided to retake the initiative. "You know, Mr. President," I said, "the Palestinians' situation grieves me terribly. They are really suffering. I was hopeful back in 2000 when you met at Camp David with President Clinton and Ehud Barak to talk peace. I watched the television all the time. I thought maybe our people would finally get their own land and enjoy a life of peace and freedom.

"But then you turned down Barak's offer. I have to tell you, I was really upset. I even threw a shoe across the room at the TV set!"

Arafat smiled. "Ah, it sounds like you haven't changed much over the years!" We both laughed to clear the air.

"Do you want to see the deal Barak offered me?" he then said. "Do you want to see what our country would have looked like?" He began spreading out a map and went into a lengthy explanation of why the peace offer was unacceptable. I listened respectfully, and when he was finished, I tried to say that, even so, a lot of world favor had been lost by his turndown.

Eventually he returned to the subject of the church. He spoke about how many civilians had been needlessly killed over the years.

"Yes, both sides have suffered many losses," I said, nodding my head. "But these are exactly the things God wants us to relieve. At the end of time, we will all stand before him, and we will have to explain our parts in these events. I ask myself sometimes what we are to say on that day."

He nodded thoughtfully.

"Mr. President," I continued, "do you know how God created man?"

"Of course. He made us from the dust of the earth."

"That is true. But have you ever considered *how* he did it?"

"Not really."

"Well, God—*al-Majid*, the Almighty, the Glorious—spoke the world into existence. He said, 'Be!' and everything took form, except for man. Then he said, 'Let us make man in our image'; that is, similar to God. In the Qur'an, too, Allah says, 'I am going to place in the earth a successor, a steward, a *khalifa*.'* This is what the Bible describes in Genesis 2.

"And when I read there how God created man, how he formed Adam's body, I suddenly got the full picture. I saw God—well, not as an actual body, but as a kind of cloud. I saw his arms moving. I saw him down on the ground, on his knees—"

"No!" Arafat interrupted. "Allah would never get down on his knees!"

I didn't argue with him. I just continued. "Mr. President, may I demonstrate it for you?"

He nodded. I rose, put my chair aside, and knelt on the floor. "This is how I saw God," I explained. "He was stretching out his hands, molding a man. Finally he leaned back a bit, looked at his work, and beamed a big smile. He had made Adam in his own image! The man was beautiful and pure; everything was right; everything was good and sound."

"Yes? Go on!" Arafat said. His eyes behind those thick glasses of his were wide open. His lips trembled all the more.

"Then God did something absolutely amazing and wonderful in my eyes."

"What did he do?"

*Sura 2:30

"God the Almighty bowed down over Adam—"

"No! Allah forbids that! Allah forbids that!" he protested. In Islam, no one bows to anyone except Allah alone. For God to bow down in the presence of a man was preposterous to Arafat.

"You know, Mr. President," I continued, "for God to do something like this must mean that he cared a great deal about humanity. I saw the next thing that happened: God put his lips on Adam's nostrils and breathed into him the breath of life. God's Spirit came into him! Suddenly, the man was alive. When I saw this, I tell you, I was shaken. Tears streamed down my face. I fell down before him and wept."

"Why is that?" Arafat wanted to know. "Why were you crying?"

"Because—if you will pardon me, Mr. President—you remember I had been a sniper. I looked people straight in the face before I took their life. I saw them through my scope. Now when I read the story of how specially God had created us, the faces of those people came back to me in a second. I felt terribly small and miserable. To take a human life that God has shaped with a great deal of effort—I felt I had passed all boundaries in doing that. I didn't even deserve to go on living myself. I wanted to die.

"But in that awful situation, something happened! I heard a voice in my ear saying, 'Despite all this, I have forgiven you.' Can you believe it, Mr. President? 'I have forgiven you'!"

I got up from my knees and sat on the chair again. I looked deep into the eyes of Yasser Arafat, this man for whom I would have once gone through fire and water. I saw tears there. "God has forgiven me. He is so merciful. He forgives us our debts. Even when we erase somebody's life, he is willing to give us inner peace.

"That is what happened to me eleven years ago. It radically changed my life.

"Now let me add something very important, if I may. Enough blood has been shed! Enough hatred has been sown. Enough is enough! Let us come to peace. And that peace comes only through Jesus, the Christ."

Arafat studied me with a careful gaze for several seconds. He then glanced aside to the two ministers who stood near the office door. It was apparent that he felt torn inside. Finally he said, "Don't go on." I could only wonder where the conversation would have led if we had been completely alone. But we were not. Other ears were listening.

A WORKING DINNER

By this time, a lot more than fifteen minutes had passed. Arafat's secretary entered the room. "Mr. President, do you need anything?" he asked, nodding in my direction. The secretary obviously wanted me to leave.

I did not want to take advantage of the situation. I knew that outside in the waiting room, many others were hoping to see this important man once I left, even at this late hour. But then Arafat said to his secretary, "This man has come all the way from America. He leaves the country tomorrow. The people outside, they live here. They can come back some other time.

"But," he continued, "let's have dinner first—all of us—and then you can send them home. I want to continue with Taysir."

Soon his staff arrived, asking us to leave the room temporarily so they could set up for dinner. Everyone but Arafat cleared the room. Ten minutes later, we were invited back. Arafat began designating who should sit where.

"Come here, sit beside me!" he motioned to me. "You sit here, and I will give you food out of my hand." This is the Arab tradition of a host who wants specifically to elevate a guest. The main plate came around. He tried each item himself, and then he urged me, "Take this! It's good! It's very good!" I was amazed at this show of honor.

Was he trying to butter me up so I would go back to America and tell people how friendly the Palestinian president was toward Christians? Was he trying to impress the others who were watching? Or was he sincerely appreciative of my visit? I couldn't tell. Maybe it was a mixture of several motives.

The meal ended at last, and the other guests left. Arafat and I continued to talk. We got back to the subject of sin and suffering.

"Do you know what the Bible says about sin?" I asked him. "Is it all right if I give you some of the details, Mr. President?"

"Oh, yes, I would love that. You know, I saw that movie *The Passion of the Christ*," he added, once again changing the subject slightly. The Mel Gibson film had just come out the previous February. "I watched it right here in my office."

"Oh, really? Then you know something about the pain and suffering the Lord Jesus Christ had to endure."

"Yes, absolutely. It was terrible how he was treated! I had never considered that before."

"So what did you think about the movie and its overall message?" I said.

"Well, it proved to me what I already knew—that *the Jews* killed the prophet Jesus!"

Ah, yes—Abu Ammar would be always looking for the political angle. I replied, "Well, there's a lot more to it than that. To go a step deeper, where do you think all the sin and hatred and revenge got started in this world in the first place?"

He didn't directly answer. All he said was, "Go on."

I talked about what Adam and Eve did to ruin paradise long ago. I talked about the Islamic tradition that a child is taken over by the devil as soon as it is born. That's why it gets slapped on the bottom—not only to clear the throat of fluids, but also to beat the devil out of the child.

"But, according to our tradition," I continued, "they didn't have to do that to Jesus, because he was the only person totally without sin, correct? That is what Muhammad taught in one of his *hadiths*: 'Satan did not touch him.'* The Bible says much the same, that he was perfect in every way."†

> Arafat and I got back to the subject of sin and suffering. "Do you know what the Bible says about sin?" I asked him.

---

*Hadith 4063
†See Hebrews 4:15.

"Very interesting," Arafat responded.

"That is why Jesus was the only person qualified to pay for our sins. He died on the cross, as it showed in the movie. And three days later, he arose."

"No, he didn't actually die on the cross," Arafat countered. "He was taken up to heaven before that could happen."

"The truth is, he *did* die," I responded.

At this moment, one of the two aides walked in and cleared his throat. He was signaling that it was surely time for me to stop preoccupying the president. It was, after all, nearly midnight.

LAST WORDS

As I rose to leave, I brought out a gift for Arafat, something I had bought in the marketplace in Cairo, where he had spent some of his early years. He received it gratefully.

"I am so glad to have met you again at this historic moment," I said. "I pray that our people will see peace during your lifetime and mine." Then I added, "Bear in mind, Mr. President, that one day you will see your Creator face to face. He will have some questions for you. What will you say then? We all must prepare to answer for what we have done."

I said this not to scare him or to manipulate him. I was speaking, after all, to a practicing Muslim. The idea of a final judgment for all humanity was well established in his frame of thinking. He knew it was a fact and would not question my motive for bringing it up.

"Yes, of course. Yes, of course." (Arafat always liked to say things twice.) He gave me a warm hug and a kiss. Then he summoned a photographer to take our picture together.

"When will these photos be ready?" I asked.

"In a week," the man said.

"Oh, but I must leave the country tomorrow," I explained.

"You make the pictures quickly," Arafat ordered the man, "so my friend can take them with him when he goes."

"Yes, Mr. President."

I then walked with him to the stairway where, after another hug and kiss, we said farewell.

I pressed a hundred dollars into the photographer's hand, saying, "Please make sure I get these pictures quickly." They would mean the world to me.

"Yes, of course," he replied.

The minister of planning added, "Bring the pictures to my office, where he can get them tomorrow before he leaves."

"Yes, Minister."

I never did get the pictures. Every inquiry was met with a reply of, "I'm working on it, I'm working on it." When time ran out, I gave him my American address. They never arrived, much to my disappointment.

I was doubly disappointed that day when, at the last minute, the appointment with Prime Minister Ariel Sharon in Jerusalem was canceled. A European delegation had arrived and wanted to see the security wall that Israel was building to keep Palestinians out. My name got bumped off the schedule.

A few months later, after I had returned home, I got a phone call from an Egyptian pastor who now lives in the United States. He had been to see Arafat a few weeks after me. "I prayed the Sinner's Prayer with him!" the pastor joyfully reported. "He confessed his sins to God and asked for forgiveness."

"Do you think he understood what was going on?" I asked.

"Yes, absolutely. He was very clear. And we were alone in the room, just the two of us."

That probably explained Arafat's willingness to go further than he had gone with me. I was glad for this new report. I sincerely hoped that it was genuine.

On November 11 of that same year, only six months after my visit, Abu Ammar died in a Paris hospital. I was in Manila that day on a ministry trip. I got the news from the television.

The whole world had been watching his decline for a week or more. When I saw that he had actually died, my heart broke. I didn't think about all that had gone astray under his leadership.

I didn't think about all the graft and misrepresentation in which he had indulged. I only thought about the man himself, now facing eternity. This was my teenage hero, the courageous leader who had dared to call the Palestinian people toward their destiny. He was the man I willingly would have died to protect.

Now he was nothing but another human being standing before an awesome God, giving answers to penetrating questions. I don't know what he said in that final court. I could only hope that in the recent months he had come to terms with the Lord of all the earth.

When I saw that he had died, my heart broke.

I grieved in my hotel room for a long time, ignoring even my meals. I prayed for the Palestinian people to find better times under new leadership. And I determined afresh to bring them the restoring news that love is stronger than hatred, that forgiveness is better than rancor, that Jesus is greater than any human politician promising victory. I wanted more than ever to bring reconciliation—God's reconciliation—to the land that Yasser Arafat had cherished so much.

CHAPTER 15

SHOWDOWN AT THE AIRPORT

AFTER THAT REMARKABLE DAY IN RAMALLAH with Yasser Arafat, I had only one more stop to make in the Middle East. I could not come this far without seeing my aged parents in Qatar. My father was now into his eighties; my mother was over seventy years old. Surely the family's anger at me would have cooled by now. After all, my conversion had happened more than a decade ago.

Karen and I had talked all this through before I left the United States. Yes, there was some risk involved. But one of God's commandments is to honor your father and mother. The Lord had protected me already through more than a few dicey situations. We prayed for his protection once again.

I made an online reservation to stay at the Gulf Hotel in Doha so I would not be an imposition on any family member. Then the day before the flight, I called my older brother, the firstborn of the family.

"Hello, this is Taysir. I am in Ramallah. I have booked a flight for tomorrow, so I can come see you and all the relatives. I want to greet our parents once again. I have not seen Mother for many years now."

"You must have a short memory, Taysir," he shot back. "Don't you recall that I want to kill you?"

Now what should I say? "Yes, I remember," I replied. "Just give me fifteen minutes. Give me time to kiss my father, my mother, and you. Then you can kill me if you like."

"Well, it's your life," he replied. "Do as you please." He promptly hung up the phone.

I dialed him right back. "Don't you want to have my flight number and arrival time?" I asked.

"Yes, of course," he answered. "You know, you really are crazy."

> I could not come this far without seeing my aged parents in Qatar.

"No, I'm not. I just have to come back and clear the air with my family. I can't leave things the way they are now. If it costs me my life, so be it." I then gave him the airline information. I told him that, unfortunately, my flight did not land until one o'clock in the morning.

He was not deterred at all. "We'll definitely be waiting for you," he said with an ominous tone.

"Thanks. I appreciate that."

When I told Karen on the phone how this conversation had gone, she was understandably fearful. She sent out a mass e-mail to all our friends to be praying for me the next day, asking God to grant me favor with my parents and siblings. That was all we could do.

INTO THE FURNACE

I could see the lights of Doha from the air. It had grown much since my last visit in 1983, becoming a real jewel of the Persian Gulf.

I landed and proceeded through customs with no delay. I walked outside the terminal into the warm night air. There I immediately saw my older brother, two younger brothers, and my older sister with her husband. My brother wore the long white caftan that is customary in Qatar and Saudi Arabia. I saw the bulge of a pistol in his pocket.

The presence of the other three men, I knew instantly, was to serve as legal witnesses for the act of honor killing. That was what Sharia law required. In just a moment, he would put the gun to my temple and ask me, "Will you turn back to Islam?" If I said no, he would ask me again. If I still said no, he would ask me a third time. Upon my third no, he would shoot me on the spot right there on the airport grounds.

And for this, he would not be prosecuted. In fact, he would be called a hero for spilling the blood of one who had befouled the family honor and insulted the family religion.

I looked at the group, and they looked at me. No words were exchanged. My heart was beating fast. I put my suitcase on the ground. Before the three questions could be uttered, I went to my older brother, kissing him on the right side of his neck. This was different from the usual kiss of greeting in our culture. This particular kiss, on the right side alone, carries a specific meaning: "I submit to your authority. I honor you. Do as you wish."

When I pulled back, I saw tears in my brother's eyes. He drew me close and hugged me. I felt his shoulders shudder as we both began to weep. We held each other for several seconds.

"Come with me," he said at last.

"You can drop me at the Gulf Hotel," I said. "I've made a reservation there."

"No, no, no," he replied. "You will stay at my house. I want you to do that."

"My brother, I should not, since I read the Bible and pray to my Lord and Savior," I explained. "It is not appropriate to do those things in your house. This could be offensive to your wife. I really do not want to insult anyone."

"What? You have dishonored the family enough already. Now you want to stay in a hotel? People will talk about us even more! You come with me. As long as you do your Bible reading in your room, it will be all right."

Things were looking better all the time.

A FATHER AND HIS SON

It was 2:30 in the morning by the time we arrived at my brother's house. We quickly went to bed, but I could not fall sleep. I first needed to thank the Lord for the favor I had received. I then prayed for more favor the next day with my parents.

I could almost predict the first question out of my mother's mouth. She was sure to ask me about whether I ate pork now that I had left Islam. Actually, I had kept to the former tradition ever since I gave my heart to the Lord, refraining from any pork or pork products.

The next morning, it was such a joy to see my parents again. We greeted each other with the traditional kiss on the back of the hand as well as the head. But then, right away, my mother said, "Taysir, do you eat pork?"

"No, Mother, I don't," I replied.

"That is good, my son," she said with a smile on her face.

We talked about my wife and children, and I gave them updates on everyone. Then my father got down to serious matters. "Why have you done this to us, my son?" he demanded, referring to my conversion.

I chose to answer with another question. "Do you think, Father, that I ignored the fact that Qatar could throw you out of the country for what I was doing? This was very much on my mind all the time. I worried about it. My Bible teaches me to honor my father and mother. Now I have come to do that."

"Oh—so you will return to Islam?"

"No, that is not what I meant. But I came all this way to see you regardless. You can kill me if you wish. Then your honor will be saved, and I will get to keep my faith. We both will win." At this, I knelt down and kissed his feet.

He leaned over to pull me back up. Relaxing a bit, he said in a gentle voice, "So tell me what happened to you."

I thought for a moment about how best to use this opening. "Father, I hope you know how strong my love for you and all my brothers and sisters is," I began. "If it were necessary, I would give my life for any of you in an instant. If I could, I would have rejected the light that came to me back in 1993 declaring, 'I am the way and the truth and the life. No one comes to the Father except through me.'"*

He had, of course, heard this story already in the long letter I had sent back then.

"I wanted for your sake to withstand this light, to dismiss it," I continued. "But it was more than I could bear. It persuaded me. The light convinced me that Jesus was the Way and the Truth. I could not help believing."

I paused for a moment to see how he was taking this.

> "You can kill me if you wish. Then your honor will be saved, and I will get to keep my faith. We both will win."

Then I said, "Do you remember Maryam, the Filipino girl who was my nanny back in Saudi Arabia? Do you remember the cross on the back of her hand? When the light talked to me, I saw *her* hands. Why did she even come into my mind? I had not seen her for such a long time, ever since we left Jiddah."

"No!" my father erupted. "Don't mention her! Curses be upon her!"

"Please don't speak badly of her," I said. "I don't know whether she is dead by now or still alive. But I know she took good care of me when I was little. I believe she was praying for me even back then."

I kept going from this point, describing in detail how Jesus had come into my life and changed me. One of my younger brothers happened to be in the room, listening to the whole discussion. Sometimes we would be crying, while at other times we would laugh about a funny thing along the way. When I finally looked at my watch, two and a half hours had passed.

My father sat there, musing to himself. Then he said, "Taysir, I think Allah has called you for a special reason."

---

*John 14:6

I was astonished. "Do you really believe that?"

"Yes, I do," he answered. "I give you my blessing."

I breathed a huge sigh of relief and began to weep with joy. The endorsement of my father would carry weight with the whole family. I didn't start a debate with him at that moment about whether Allah had called me as opposed to the one true God. I simply accepted the welcome back into the family, knowing that further discussions were now possible.

I stayed in Qatar a full week. Some of my brothers and their wives came to see me after hearing what my father had said. Others, however, kept their distance. I went to my older sister's home to show respect to her. The atmosphere was somewhat stiff there. I got a similar chilly reception when I visited old friends from school days. I tried to remain loving regardless.

Back at my oldest brother's house, he would try to persuade me to change my mind about Christianity. I had actually prayed for this kind of opportunity because it allowed me to reply with explanations of Christ as the only way.

When the time came to leave, the tension was obvious among the family. I could tell they had hoped to convince me during this visit to return to Islam. Instead, I was leaving the country with my faith intact—as well as my life!

On the plane home, I thought to myself, *So this is what it's like when believers stand together in intercession for one another.* My friends back at Heartland and across America had fervently asked God to grant me favor in this place. That prayer had been dramatically answered. I could only praise God for his goodness to me.

I was leaving the country with my faith intact—as well as my life!

When I phoned my mother a couple of days later, she told me of a family meeting that took place after my departure. Several were angry with my oldest brother for not carrying out the honor killing. But my father had spoken up to say, "I have blessed Taysir now. Anyone in this family who curses him, I will curse." At this, the room got very quiet. No one dared to criticize me or my faith after that.

BACK TO MY ROOTS

When I returned to Israel the next year (2005), I was determined to get into the Gaza Strip—my birthplace. I stayed with some Messianic friends in the Israeli port city of Ashdod, about twenty-two miles north. From there I called an American-Palestinian friend who lives in Gaza, asking if he could come see me. When he arrived, I told him about my desire.

"Do you have a permit?" he asked right away.

"What kind of permit?"

"You have to have an Israeli permit to get into the Strip the first time," he explained. "And the process usually takes a week to ten days."

This was a setback I hadn't anticipated.

"Well, how about if I go with you to the checkpoint tomorrow and just talk to them?" I said. "It can't hurt to try."

He smiled at my naiveté. But he was willing to escort me there. We prayed together that night for favor, and when I talked with Karen I asked her to get others praying, too.

We arrived the next morning at the Erez checkpoint on the north end of the Gaza Strip. It is an amazing complex. Israeli military personnel are everywhere, of course. You get screened on both sides of the border. In between is a winding, twisting tunnel about a half-mile long, just to make sure you don't try to rush across. Getting through airport security in the United States is a cakewalk compared to this place. Yet even so, Erez has been jolted more than once by terrorist attacks.

> He smiled at my naiveté. But he was willing to escort me there.

I approached the first counter with my passport. The soldier took a quick look and then said, "Do you have the permit as well?"

"No, I'm sorry, I don't."

"Well, then I can't let you through," she answered. She was not mean about it, but her word was firm. She took an extra minute to cross-check a list of passports that had received clearance.

"Don't bother," I said. "I'm sure my name is not there."

"Didn't you even give advanced notification?"

"No, I didn't."

She looked up. "Well, then definitely we can't let you in," she concluded.

I decided to try the personal approach. "Actually, I was hoping to go across for just an hour or two. I was born here many years ago, but my family left for Saudi Arabia only two months later. So I've never been back to visit. I just want to see where I was born, and then leave."

I could tell she wanted to accommodate me. But her only words were, "You need to register in Tel Aviv. That's the first step."

I then said, "Is there someone in charge to whom I could speak?"

"Yes, of course," she replied. Soon she had arranged for me to speak with her supervisor in his office.

I was surprised when the Israeli officer greeted me not in English but in Arabic. He spoke it fluently.

"You speak my language better than I do, and I'm an Arab!" I said.

He laughed. "Well, I grew up here," he explained. "How can I help you?"

I went through my story again. I pled for just one hour to look around. He was compassionate as he answered, "Ooh, I really wish I could help you. But I'm not authorized. I'm sorry, but my hands are tied."

"Thank you for being willing," I said. "Who around here would have the authority to help?"

"Maybe the top officer," he said. "Shall I call him?"

"Yes, please do."

He phoned his superior and began to speak in Hebrew, which I, of course, could not understand. A short while later, the man walked into this office to greet me. "Come with me!" he said in good English, leading me toward his office.

"What can I do for you?"

I went through my situation for the third time. He listened carefully.

Then he said, "Are you with a Palestinian organization? Or have you ever worked in one?"

"Yes. I was once in Fatah. I was a fighter with them."

"Oh, were you?" he said with surprise at my candor. "What precisely did you do?"

"I was trained for guerrilla warfare. In fact, I was a sniper."

"Are you serious, or are you just pulling my leg?" he wanted to know. He couldn't believe that I would admit this.

"I'm entirely serious," I said. "There's no use trying to hide something from you, is there?"

"No, no. I'm glad you are being honest with me."

Seeing that I had his trust, I figured I might as well keep going. "But let me add something else," I continued. "You know, twelve years ago something happened to me that turned my life around. Before that, I could not have sat in this office without thinking of how I might kill you. But now, do you know what I'm thinking here?"

"What?"

"I'm thinking about how to love you in the best way. You see, my eyes were opened by Jesus Christ. Suddenly I could distinguish good from evil. I realized I had been fighting the wrong kind of war. You Israelis do have a right to this land, and I had been trying to take what rightfully belongs to you. My life isn't the same anymore. Every day I pray for the Jewish people."

"Hmm, this is certainly unusual," he said. He paused for a moment, then asked, "Are you with some kind of organization now?"

"Yes, I am. It is called 'Hope for Ishmael.' I am the founder, in fact."

"What do you do?" he asked.

"We're a humanitarian organization. We try to help both Palestinians and Jews come to reconcile with God and with each other."

"That's very interesting," he said. "I don't know why, but . . .

I think I should help you today. Do you have any brochures or booklets describing your work?"

"Just a minute," I said. I went outside his office to where my friend patiently waited with my briefcase. I returned with some Hope for Ishmael material for the officer to see. He looked it over, then handed me an application form for entry into the Gaza Strip.

"Fill this out," he said, "and we'll fax it to Tel Aviv. Who knows what will happen? An answer could come back in two hours . . . or six, or eight . . . or not till tomorrow. Are you willing to wait?"

"Yes, of course," I replied.

When I handed him the completed form, he added a couple of things in Hebrew. That made me nervous.

"What did you write?" I asked him.

"Just that I recommend they let you enter, since you're in humanitarian work."

"Thank you very much," I said. "You have been most helpful."

FIRST GLIMPSE

My friend and I sat waiting after this, watching people come and go. There wasn't much to occupy our attention. An hour passed, then an hour and a half.

Sometime around noon, the second officer I had spoken to came over to where we were sitting. He had a fax in his hand. He looked at me strangely, shaking his head.

"Did they turn me down?" I asked.

"No! You are cleared to enter. In fact, they've even registered your organization as a humanitarian entity. That means you can go back and forth into Gaza as much as you wish. You can even bring people with you, provided they get permits through Tel Aviv."

I was close to tears in this moment. The officer continued, "You know what? I've been working here three years, and I've never seen something like this. You must have someone up there taking care of you!"

"I do!" I replied. "I really do!"

My friend and I soon walked through the tunnel and out onto Gaza soil. We hailed a taxi to take us on a tour. People and buses and donkey carts and private cars all jostled against one another in the crowded streets. Bullet holes were everywhere. The roads were scarred with tank tracks. Everywhere we looked reminded us of a war zone.

We asked to see the city of Rafah down in the south, where the Israelis had been demolishing buildings in search of tunnels that went across to Egypt. At least, that's what the media had been reporting. We expected to see mass destruction.

When we got there, we saw much less damage. Yes, certain buildings very close to the border had been flattened—but right next to them were others standing intact. The surgical precision of the IDF (Israel Defense Forces) bombs amazed me.

We then asked the taxi driver to take us to al-Breij, the camp where I was born. There were no more tents, of course, but the mud-brick houses jammed on top of each other were hardly a great improvement. The population density in this place took my breath away. The noise of car horns and vendors with loudspeakers was constant. Machine guns chattered in the background, and people hardly seemed to take notice.

I pulled out my cell phone and called my mother. "You will never believe where I'm standing right now!" I said to her. "I'm in Gaza at the camp of my birth. Can you give me directions to where we lived?" She began telling me how to walk and where to turn. Eventually she guided me to the very spot where our tent had been pitched fifty-four years before. It was now a school.

I began talking to people in the street there. I told them I had been born in this very place long ago. I told them my family had come from Jaffa.

"Yes," said an old man, "this was the area where people from Jaffa all clustered together back then. You could walk from one section to another and more or less change hometowns as you went along."

I had no conscious memories of this place since our family had left when I was only two months old. Still, these were my roots. Here was where life began for me. And sadly, life today was little better than it had been so long ago.

I looked into the faces of the children in the street. They seemed tough, hardened before their time. There was no gentleness here that I could see, no human compassion. There was only resentment and the thirst for revenge.

I thought of the children I had once trained for guard duty back in the Jordanian camps. These Gaza kids now seemed even tougher than my little "army" back then. I knew they were being indoctrinated at school, incited by television programs, and radicalized by imams at the mosque. What havoc would they inflict as they grew up?

Here was where life began for me. And sadly, life today was little better than it had been so long ago.

My friend and I got back into the taxi and headed for the border crossing. By evening, we were back in Ashdod. I was strongly affected by what I had seen. My thoughts were not so much about my family heritage as about the needs of the present. What could I do to bring hope to this desolate landscape?

In July and August 2005, I was back again. This was during that time of great controversy when the Israeli government was demanding that Jewish settlers leave the Gaza Strip, so it could then wash its hands of having to administer the territory. Nine thousand people were forced to give up their homes. I saw their pain and rage. I also saw the discomfort on the faces of the IDF soldiers as they were ordered to use force against their own people.

Meanwhile, many Palestinians were upset, too, fearing what would happen when the Israeli police and military were gone. Would the Palestinian Authority be able to maintain control? Or would the Strip descend into worse chaos? These thoughts were dangerous to express, of course. Nobody would speak frankly to the media. But down inside, they churned.

A CALLING?

I came home once again with much to share with my wife. I told her all about the turmoil of Gaza. I described how the children were having their innocence snatched away at such a young age. "Somehow, Karen, I feel we should go and work there. I don't think this is just nostalgia. Gaza needs people who will work for peace, for forgiveness, for reconciliation."

She was apprehensive about the thought of leaving our comfortable home at Heartland, of course. She remembered her earlier time in Qatar back in the 1980s and how hard it had been to cross the cultural barriers. But she also heard me when I talked about the dire needs of people trapped in hopelessness. She was willing to do whatever God asked us to do.

Early in the new year (2006) we went back to Israel together. We attended a business conference in Haifa, and we also spent ten days staying in Gaza itself. We tried to imagine ourselves living there. We talked to many people. We got acquainted with those at the Palestinian Bible Society and attended the Gaza Baptist Church. We let our hearts be broken by the fate of the children especially.

"But do we need to *live* here?" Karen asked. "Could we accomplish just as much if we lived in, say, Jerusalem, and you commuted here? It's not that far."

I saw her point. That would certainly be easier on us personally.

But the longer we prayed, the more we sensed that we were called by God to live in Gaza itself. We needed to immerse ourselves in the desperate needs of these streets. We saw how badly they needed ministries not all that different from Heartland's—a school for children, sustainable businesses to relieve the grinding unemployment, fellowship groups that could meet in homes and help strengthen the tiny Christian community. Karen was with me, confirming that if this was God's place for us, we should take the plunge.

When my family in Qatar heard what we were thinking, they were amazed. They tried to talk me out of it, actually. I thought it was curious that my oldest brother, who once was intent on killing me, now spoke like a counselor and protector of his little brother.

"You're doing something I could never do," he said on the phone. "My wife would never go for living in Gaza! But you say that your wife agrees?"

"Yes. She is willing to follow the direction of God," I replied.

"Then God be with you. I give you my blessing." I could hardly believe my ears.

Somehow I sensed that Karen and I had been in training for this moment for a very long time.

CHAPTER 16

BACK
TO
THE
BARRICADES

IT FELT STRANGE TO BE MOVING BACK into the thick of Middle Eastern conflict—with a wife to protect, no less—and not have a single pistol or AK-47 at my disposal. This was definitely not the way I had operated in the same environment years ago. Then, I had been among the few who were armed to the teeth. Now, I had no armaments—and everybody around me had plenty.

Karen and I were in a position perhaps best described by the apostle Paul when he wrote, "Though we live in the world, we do not wage war as the world does. The weapons we fight with are not the weapons of the world. On the contrary, they have divine power."* We were coming to the barricades of mistrust and hatred and revenge with only the weapons of love and kindness and practical service.

We rented a large house in the village of Khou'zah, down in the southeast part—although nothing in the Gaza Strip is too far away from anything else. The whole territory is only thirty-four miles long and an average of five miles wide. With a total land area of just 139 square miles, it is one-eighth the size of Rhode Island.

---

*2 Corinthians 10:3-4

Yet 1.6 million Palestinians are packed into the area, making it almost as jammed as Hong Kong or Singapore—but without the economic resources and infrastructure to handle the crush.

Our house had five bedrooms, which gave us enough space to host small groups, conduct training classes, and receive volunteers who might come to work with us. Looking east, we could see across the electric-fence border to Israeli land, where farmers were busy cultivating their wheat and corn with powerful tractors and other modern equipment. On our side, Palestinians were tilling their land with horse-drawn plows and bending their backs to harvest crops by hand. In the city streets, people scrambled to stay alive by making souvenirs and carvings, or selling sandwiches and cigarettes.

> **Then, I had been among the few who were armed to the teeth. Now, I had no armaments—and everybody around me had plenty.**

The neighbors weren't quite sure what to think of us at first. Some said we might be spies for the Israelis—or for America's CIA. We could only tell them we had no government connections and had come at our own expense to try to help Gazans. Only time would prove we were telling the truth.

In the pressure cooker Gaza has become, this kind of suspicion and distorted thinking simmers readily. It is truly a tragedy. People's feelings are on edge all the time. Anger can boil over for the smallest reason, or none at all. Not even every faction of the PLO is in agreement: Hamas, the more hard-line group, is recognized as a terrorist organization and is opposed to Fatah's more secular, comparatively moderate nationalism. We witnessed fights breaking out constantly—even at a funeral. When two Fatah members were gunned down by their rivals in Hamas and were being mourned, some Hamas activists wanted to attend the service. At the graveside, an argument turned into a gun battle. One person died; fourteen others were wounded.

On a different day, no more than 500 meters (about 550 yards) from our house, a father, mother, and their children—all in full battle gear—decided to block the road as a method of getting back at another family.

On top of this, the Israeli army was conducting strikes into Gaza at all hours of the day. Some were long-range bombing operations, but more often they would use Black Hawk helicopters with rockets to attack certain buildings or automobiles that might house terrorists. They also parked a tank across the border—we could see it from our rooftop—to shoot "noise bombs" throughout the day as a scare tactic or warning to subversive groups in the area. The bombs didn't harm anything; they just sounded as if they would.

Early one morning in August 2006, before the usual noise bomb went off about two miles away, Karen awoke to the sound of gunfire much closer. It was being returned with other gunfire that sounded different than usual. She woke me up. I quickly dressed and ran up to the roof of our house to see what I could learn.

There I saw a full-scale street battle underway between Israeli soldiers and masked Hamas gunmen—all being filmed by an Al Jazeera TV network cameraman in a black jacket! I ran back down the stairs and out the front door. I'm sure Karen wanted to caution me to stay inside, but I was too quick for her. I began shouting to the gunmen, "Get out of our neighborhood!" Soon neighbors came out of their houses to reinforce the message.

Amazingly, the gunmen started backing up. We chased them down the road. They motioned to the cameraman to meet them on another street a block away. The gunshots did not subside until about four o'clock that afternoon. An ambulance came down our street at one point, trying to pick up the injured.

It was a tense day, and not the last battle to happen in front of our home. Two weeks later, another skirmish erupted. My family in Qatar saw the news story and even recognized our house. They began frantically trying to phone to see if we were all right. Fortunately, we were not home for this episode; we had left for some speaking engagements in Switzerland. When we returned a few days later, we found two bullet holes in the front gate and the wall of our bedroom.

No wonder Karen, who does not speak Arabic, felt constrained to stay indoors. She did not complain, however. We simply kept our focus on what God had asked us to do, which was to lift up the spirits and hopes of these people, to let them know that they were not abandoned to violence and terror. Somebody cared. And why did we care? Because of the love that Jesus Christ had placed in our hearts.

REFUGE FOR THE YOUNG

Our first effort was to raise up Hope Kindergarten. We found a suitable building in the village with a large yard where we could install swings, a slide, and other play equipment. It was shaded by several olive trees. We got busy hiring staff, and when we opened in September 2006, we had sixty students. Parents thanked us profusely for giving their little ones a safe and positive place to spend their mornings.

By planting seeds of hope in these precious children, we felt we were neutralizing the hatred that would otherwise surely take root as they grew up. They were learning that revenge must not have the last word. They were seeing the value of building instead of destroying, of learning about the wider world instead of continuing in ignorance. They were finding that at least some adults in their community could be trusted, not feared.

All of this required a good deal of money, naturally. God provided funds from a wide variety of sources—even a grant from the government of Finland. From time to time we would have to make short trips back to the United States for more fund-raising. But our hearts always longed to get back to Gaza.

Next we launched Seeds of Hope Cultural Learning Center for young people, with classes on everything from computer skills to English to a unique course entitled Democracy, Tolerance, and Peace. Some sixty adults signed up for that first class, representing twenty different humanitarian organizations. The community response was tremendous.

We built relationships with three nearby Internet cafés that would employ the students we had trained. In areas of the world where most people are too poor to own their own computers, the neighborhood Internet café is a vital access point for them. Especially in Gaza, where travel is restricted, this is practically the only way to find out what's going on in the larger world. We wanted a part in this endeavor as well.

Meanwhile, we were making contacts with what are discreetly described as "MBBs" (Muslim-background believers) throughout the Gaza Strip, inviting them to our house for Bible classes taught by not only us but also several outside instructors. We held the sessions on Friday, the Islamic holy day when the students would not be at work (if they were fortunate enough even to have a job). They arrived around 10:00 a.m., and instruction lasted until 1:00 p.m., when we would break for a hearty lunch prepared by Karen. The fellowship was greatly appreciated by all. We called it our "Bible college."

> By planting seeds of hope in these precious children, we were neutralizing the hatred that would otherwise surely take root as they grew up.

The more MBBs we met, the more amazing stories we heard. So many had come to faith in Christ because of a powerful dream in the night. One was a twenty-two-year-old former Hamas member who had volunteered to be a suicide bomber—until Jesus showed up one night while he slept. It reminded me of what God said through the prophet Isaiah: "I revealed myself to those who did not ask for me; I was found by those who did not seek me. To a nation that did not call on my name, I said, 'Here am I, here am I.'"*

To political leaders who want to dominate the population, of course, this kind of thing is exasperating. They can cut off evangelistic events and broadcasting, they can limit travel, they can root out copies of the Bible—but what can they do about a dream in which Jesus appears to a person asleep at home and says, "Come, follow me"? God's message of love and forgiveness gets through the most determined blockade.

---

*Isaiah 65:1

On August 20, we baptized five new believers in the Mediterranean. We had offered to do it more quietly in our home, using a bathtub. But they insisted on being baptized in the open. We spent a long time afterward sitting there on the beach, talking about how important Christ had become to us all. A bond was forged among us that day that would not soon be forgotten.

WAR ZONE

It was a good thing that so much groundwork was laid during our first year in Gaza—because in June 2007 the political situation changed dramatically. The "unity government" of Fatah and Hamas, which had been tottering for some seventeen months, fell apart at last, erupting in a fierce battle for supremacy.

Hamas makes no secret of its goal to obliterate Israel by any means possible. More extremist than Fatah, Hamas is uninterested in diplomatic maneuvers. It criticizes Fatah for being halfhearted as well as corrupt. The more damage that Hamas leaders can inflict to destabilize the situation and scare away tourists from the region, the happier they are. Peace talks and peace plans are, in Hamas's viewpoint, a joke.

My wife and I, mercifully, were out of the Gaza Strip when the guns began blazing on June 7. For a week, the two sides tried to obliterate each other. One Fatah officer was thrown off the top of Gaza's tallest building, a fifteen-story apartment high-rise. A few hours later, Fatah threw a captured Hamas militant off a twelve-story building. By June 15, Fatah was in retreat, and Hamas had prevailed. They were the "new boss" up and down the Gaza Strip. This would certainly make life more tenuous for anyone with a mind for peace or reconciliation.

Nevertheless, we could not just pull away from those we had been called to serve. Our staff pushed ahead with a two-week summer camp for elementary-age kids in the village, giving them something positive to focus on instead of all the strife. As the children played games and did crafts, parents told us how grateful they were. In fact, we filled up to maximum capacity and had to turn some away for lack of room.

As soon as I was able to reenter Gaza, I began working with the new leadership as best I could, emphasizing that our organization only wanted to help the local people. We were able to partner with an international aid organization to bring food to needy families. We distributed four thousand boxes of food to the very poor, including those in the al-Breij camp where I was born. Each box would feed a family of five for a week. We also managed to give out four thousand backpacks filled with school supplies.

Hope Kindergarten opened on schedule that September for its second year of operation, with ninety-eight students this time. One Tuesday afternoon after the children had gone home, about twenty Hamas gunmen in masks rolled up to the school in two trucks. They broke down the door, intending to ransack the place.

Word spread quickly through the village. Within minutes, parents came running to intervene. "What do you think you're doing?" they shouted at the intruders. "This is *our* school. This is doing something good for *our* children. Why is it that every time we have the start of a good chance for our children, you try to destroy it?!"

"We are just looking for a suspect," the soldiers tried to say. "A young man has been picking up girls and taking them on 'dates' to this school."

"That is nonsense, and you know it," the headmaster retorted. "You are only trying to destroy our school because it is funded by foreign money, and you don't want us to have anything good."

The crowd in the street began to demand, "Come out! Take off your masks! Show your faces! Leave our school!"

And to their amazement, the fierce Hamas intruders backed down. The kindergarten was left unharmed, ready to welcome children the next morning and keep teaching.

FULL CIRCLE

Whenever Karen and I would leave the Gaza Strip for any short trip, it would be harder and harder to gain reentry. More than once we had to bide our time elsewhere. We often went to the West

Bank. This area, still under Fatah control, was more accessible to us than the Gaza Strip had now become.

We began to sense the Lord's nudging that we might minister to Palestinians here as well. What if we were to start a parallel kindergarten and youth center in Jericho? We began meeting people in the local churches, including a Christian family who hosted weekly meetings in the restaurant they owned. In these meetings, we saw how many Muslim women were willing to attend for the benefit of receiving free milk that was given away.

In January 2008, we could not get back into the Gaza Strip at all. It was extremely frustrating to be stopped just a few miles from where our staff was working faithfully under trying circumstances. We needed to be with them; we needed to bring them fresh funding.

Once again, we diverted to Jericho. We prayed that God might show us a suitable building to rent. The third one we inspected was on the side of a hill with four different levels and a number of rooms that could be used for classes. The layout seemed to be perfect for our purposes.

The landlord took us up to the rooftop for a view of the city. He began pointing out various landmarks on the horizon. Then he said, "And over there to the east you see al-Karameh. . . ."

We began to sense the Lord's nudging that we might minister to Palestinians here as well.

"What?!" I interrupted him. "What did you say? Al-Karameh?"

"Yes, right over there across the river."

I looked at my wife with amazement. I had not even thought about the fact that I was back in the vicinity of the dramatic battle of March 1968. This was the place where so long ago I had come to fight and take life. Now, God was bringing me back to do good and give life. What a confirmation of the Lord's direction!

The financial negotiations with the man went smoothly—even better than we had expected. We signed the paperwork and began making plans for future ministry in that building. I had come full circle after forty years, sent to bring God's peace to a troubled land. I could never have planned this turn of events. But God knew what he was doing. He had a purpose for us in this place as well as in Gaza.

CHAPTER 17

BEHIND THE CURTAIN

THE MORE TIME I SPEND IN THE MIDDLE EAST these days, the more I come to see what is going on behind the scenes—and has been for many years. Reality is sometimes hard to track as long as you live in America or another part of the world. But when you are up close to the action, you start to notice the subtle things.

For example, consider the stunning collapse of the Arab forces in the Six-Day War of 1967, back when I was just a teenager. I had sat by the radio gleefully tallying the number of Israeli planes shot down—all the way up to 720—and then I found out the truth. I was so angry. That moment was the catalyst that started me toward becoming a Fatah fighter myself.

Why did this shameful defeat occur? Well, for one thing, we Arabs had picked the wrong arms supplier. The Soviets didn't really care about our fight with Israel. They merely saw an opportunity to have someone else try out their weapons in a real-life field test. From our experience, they could see how well their armaments performed. Their instructors had taught the Egyptians and Syrians how to use the equipment . . . but then they seemed to disappear once the fighting began. They didn't stick around to give advice during the heat of battle.

Fiery public speeches by Arab politicians of the day were a long way from the lukewarm motivation the various Arab armies brought to the actual battlefields. They had little ambition to try to win. They certainly didn't want to incorporate Palestinian fighters into their ranks for fear of where Palestinian loyalties might lie in the end. Everybody was too busy concocting conspiracy theories to concentrate on the job at hand.

The only exception to this malaise was the Iraqi military, which fought valiantly, just as they had in 1948. This pattern continued right up through the time of Saddam Hussein. His disdain for Israel was backed up by hard-hitting missile strikes. That is why he was always popular in the Palestinian community. We knew little, of course, about how harshly he treated his own people.

The truth of the matter is, it's not accurate to say the Jews turned us into refugees. We left our homes because the Arab governments advised us to do so, making way for a campaign they assured us they would win—but then didn't. We were taken in by a lie. Once we uprooted ourselves at their behest, there would be no replanting.

DID THEY OR DIDN'T THEY?

Yasser Arafat's promises at the 1993 Oslo peace talks were another example of deceitful dealings. There in the first-ever face-to-face negotiations between the PLO and Israel, he promised that the PLO charter would be changed to remove all calls for the destruction of Israel. The world beamed in appreciation, even giving him (along with Yitzhak Rabin and Shimon Peres) the Nobel Peace Prize the next year.

The only trouble was, the charter did not get changed. In November 1995, Rabin paid with his life for trying to work with Arafat, struck down by an assassin. Shimon Peres then set an ultimatum that the change must happen by March 1996, or all further talks would stop. Arafat said he would keep his promise.

It wasn't until April 24, 1996, that the 669 members of the

Palestine National Council (PNC) met to discuss charter language. After a short debate, 504 voted for altering the articles that called for Israel's destruction. Or so it was reported. Actually, the motion was rather *to convey the matter to a new legislation committee* of the PNC, which would bring the matter to a future meeting of the full body on a date not yet determined.

Shimon Peres was delighted to receive a letter from Yasser Arafat stating that "the charter has been changed." At least, that is what the translation appeared to say. The original Arabic text, however, said, "It has been decided that the charter will be changed"—a statement of intent but not actual fact. Meanwhile, internal Fatah minutes stated clearly that the Palestinian charter remained as it had always been, with no changes whatsoever.

The world figured this out eventually. When Israel elected a new conservative prime minister, Benjamin Netanyahu, in 1997, he demanded that the PLO finally keep its leader's word. The uncertainty continued for the rest of that year and the year following. US President Bill Clinton even showed up for a PNC meeting on December 14, 1998, where an enthusiastic show of hands voted to "endorse the decision" to change the charter. Again, the world's headlines rejoiced. However, many of the affirmative voters that day were not actually PNC members but members of other Palestinian groups. So the vote was flawed and carried no official weight.

As late as January 23, 2002—nearly a decade after the Oslo talks—Zuhair Sanduka, director of the PNC's parliamentary affairs department, admitted, "No other charter has indeed been written." The world had been purposely deceived and strung along the whole time.

This pattern of finessing the truth, of saying one thing but doing another, is epidemic in Middle Eastern politics. It explains why progress is often so excruciatingly slow. It also illustrates the desperate need on all levels, from high government halls to the common street, to speak honestly and accurately about one's intentions.

There is a cultural problem here, in that lying is viewed within Islam as an acceptable tactic if it advances the goals of the religion.

To help the cause of Allah by misleading an infidel is perfectly noble. Thus, Arab leaders are infamous for duplicity with Israel and the Western nations.

In fact, they even practice it among themselves. Tribal and national interests lead to jealousy and mistrust. Some of the ethnic groups are Ishmaelites, and others are not. The Egyptians, for example, trace their lineage back to Noah's son Ham, even though they speak Arabic today. When pressure of any kind comes, the temptation to think in terms of "us" and "them" proves irresistible, and duplicity characterizes the negotiations.

This pattern of finessing the truth, of saying one thing but doing another, is epidemic in Middle Eastern politics.

I have seen ordinary people in the tiny Gaza Strip squabbling with one another because of their different heritages. If the Arab peoples could join together in a common cause, they would accomplish far more than they do now with all their infighting. But the lack of truthfulness holds them back.

WHAT IS GOD THINKING?

Further behind the curtain in this Middle Eastern drama lies a spiritual dimension that is beyond human peculiarities. I am convinced, from my reading of Scripture, that God wants the Jews to be living in this land. He promised it to them long ago through his prophets, and he has never changed his mind on that.

So to try to throw them out is to fight against God. That is why we Arabs, in spite of our larger numbers, our petrodollars, and all the rest, have never been able to defeat Israel.

Yes, I know this view will not be popular with my people—or with Jews, either. The Israelis prefer to think that they've beaten us because they are tough and smart and courageous on their own. That is true, but it's not the whole story. Meanwhile, we Arabs don't like thinking that God is against our military efforts. We find that to be patently unfair.

The truth is, God loves both Arabs and Jews—and wants to bring us both to a higher perspective. He is not "anti" either one of us. He wants the peoples of the Middle East, *all* of us, to realize that Jesus is our Savior and Reconciler.

We have both fallen short of our divine destinies. We Arabs have stood in opposition to God's plan for the Jews, hurting many thousands of innocent people along the way. But the Jews have also failed to follow their calling. God called them to be "a light for the Gentiles, that you may bring my salvation to the ends of the earth,"* said the prophet many centuries ago. They have not done so.

At nearly the same time in history, God gave the Jews a grand vision of how to relate to their neighbors. Ezekiel prophesied that land should be allotted on a broad scale:

"'You are to distribute this land among yourselves according to the tribes of Israel. You are to allot it as an inheritance for yourselves"—(don't stop reading yet!)—"and for the aliens who have settled among you and who have children. You are to consider them as native-born Israelites; along with you they are to be allotted an inheritance among the tribes of Israel. In whatever tribe the alien settles, there you are to give him his inheritance,' declares the Sovereign LORD."†

> We have both fallen short of our divine destinies.

Could any instruction be more clear—or more bold? God is saying that the Holy Land was meant for Jews and non-Jews to enjoy *together*. No one was to be considered a second-class citizen. The land was meant to be a common inheritance.

This is not an impossible dream after all. It is a calling from above.

I have heard some Christians thoughtlessly say, "God brought his chosen people back to the Holy Land in 1948, and Satan built up his nations all around to withstand them." That is one of the silliest things I've ever heard. It ignores the fact that God is the Father of us all. He loves Isaac—and he loves Ishmael as well. In fact, more

---

*Isaiah 49:6
†Ezekiel 47:21-23. *Alien* here has also been translated *foreigner*.

and more Muslims, especially Ishmaelites, are coming to find the Lord. The numbers are increasing rapidly. More and more groups of Arabic-speaking Christians are forming all the time across the Middle East. Meanwhile, Jews up and down the nation of Israel are also discovering their Messiah.

The reconciliation that God has in mind for the peoples of the Middle East is grander and more far-reaching than almost any human being can imagine. It is fair to both sides. And it is a mission that should drive our efforts in his name.

But what does this quest for peace require of us?

PART 3

ROAD
MAP
TO
RECONCILIATION

CHAPTER 18

FOR
THE
MIDDLE
EAST

WHEREVER I GO TO SPEAK THESE DAYS, whether in America, Europe, or the Middle East, audiences have one earnest question to ask me. It comes in a variety of phrasings, but it always goes to the heart of the matter:

"So, Tass, what really is the solution for this conflict? How can the Jews and the Arabs ever get along?"

This dilemma has occupied the world's attention for more than half a century now. Thousands have been killed, hundreds of thousands injured, millions displaced. We are now seeing the fourth generation poisoned by the ongoing bitterness. Israel is obliged to spend huge amounts of money it doesn't have as it tries to secure its people, only to be shocked again and again by terrorist strikes. At the same time, my people are suffering the loss of dignity and hope for any kind of future, not to mention the retaliatory deaths when Israel hits back with its fearsome arsenal.

Politicians and pundits give continuing lip service to the idea of a Palestinian homeland, but nobody can define what it would look like. President George W. Bush said it must not be "a piece of Swiss cheese," with Israeli enclaves interrupting the continuity. The alternatives, however, are even less acceptable. Will my family ever get its Jaffa orange grove back? Obviously not. Then what would be fair compensation? And who could afford it? No one knows.

Wherever I go to speak, audiences have one earnest question to ask me: "How can the Jews and the Arabs ever get along?"

World leaders strive mightily to untangle this terrible knot; they fantasize about crowning their legacies with success where so many before them have failed. President Jimmy Carter brought Anwar Sadat of Egypt and Menachem Begin of Israel together for thirteen dramatic days at Camp David back in 1978. Twenty-two years later, President Bill Clinton returned to the same location with Yasser Arafat and Ehud Barak. In recent times, U.S. Secretary of State Condoleezza Rice has gone on numerous Middle East peace missions. Great Britain's Prime Minister Tony Blair, upon leaving office in 2007, was named official United Nations envoy to the Middle East.

And still the rockets scream. Still the innocent die. Still the hatred boils.

A PEACE PLAN LIKE NO OTHER

I believe that if there were a political answer for this awful deadlock, some bright statesman or scholar would have thought of it by now. While I appreciate all the time, money, travel, and deliberation that have been invested, my personal view is that mere diplomacy is simply not going to solve this. Summit conferences and congressional hearings and UN Security Council resolutions will not achieve the breakthrough for which we all yearn.

Neither is war going to settle the matter. The Israelis have won several wars, but peace has not come. The Palestinians are not going to just "go away." And neither are the Jews, obviously. Neither side has the power to subdue the other.

With all my heart I do believe, however, that peace is still possible. The bitterness and resentment can be softened if we will do four things.

1. We must understand that the house of Ishmael has a divine purpose, too.

We Ishmaelites—Arab descendants of Ishmael—were never intended by God to be outcasts or pariahs. I wrote in an earlier chapter about God's strong promise to Abraham about his firstborn: "I will surely bless him; I will make him fruitful and will greatly increase his numbers. He will be the father of twelve rulers, and I will make him into a great nation."* Even when Abraham's family exploded in tension, and he felt he needed to banish Ishmael with his mother, God repeated his vow: "I will make the son of the maidservant into a nation also, because he is your offspring."†

In fact, Ishmael grew up to become the father of precisely twelve sons. Their names are listed twice in the Bible: Nebaioth, Kedar, Abdeel, Mibsam, and so forth.‡ These names aren't nearly as familiar to most churchgoers, of course, as the twelve grandsons of Isaac who became the twelve tribes of Israel (Reuben, Simeon, Levi, Judah, etc.). But that doesn't mean they should be ignored. In fact, the prophecies of Isaiah twice refer to two of Ishmael's sons—and in a positive light. Isaiah 42:11 invites "the settlements where Kedar lives" to join in singing a new song to the Lord. Isaiah 60:7 predicts that someday "Kedar's flocks will be gathered" and "the rams of Nebaioth" will all be part of a joyous festival in God's house. We can hardly imagine such a thing, can we? Yet that is what God said through his prophet.

Today in our century, if you want to count Ishmaelites, you will arrive at twelve groupings:

> The Saudis (some of whom drifted northward to become
> the Palestinians)
> The Jordanians

---

*Genesis 17:20
†Genesis 21:13
‡See Genesis 25:12-18 and 1 Chronicles 1:29-31.

The Iraqis

The Kuwaitis

The Qataris

The seven sheikdoms of the United Arab Emirates: Dubai,
Abu Dhabi, Àjman, Fujairah, Ras al-Khaimah, Sharjah,
and Umm al-Qaiwain

I am not claiming there is a one-to-one correlation of these twelve people groups with the twelve sons of Ishmael long ago. I just think it is interesting that the number twelve perseveres to this day in Ishmaelite demographics.

These names aren't nearly as familiar to most churchgoers as the twelve grandsons of Isaac. But that doesn't mean they should be ignored.

And if you add up all the ethnic Ishmaelites in these nations plus those in the Gaza Strip and the West Bank, you come to some fifty-eight million—a "greatly increased number," as God put it back in Genesis.* The purely Jewish population of neighboring Israel, by contrast, is less than a tenth of that—around five million.

All through the centuries, through good times and bad, the Ishmaelites have remained free. No power has been able to enslave them. Granted, their lands have been occupied for certain periods (during the British mandate, for example). But these people have never really submitted to outside domination.

In that, they have fulfilled what was promised to Hagar: that her son would be "a wild donkey of a man."† When I first read that, I was furious! How dare the angel of the Lord call my ancestor a donkey? What an insult! Then I calmed down and did some research. I learned that it referred to "probably the onager, which roamed the dry steppes of the Near East."[1] This animal was a fitting metaphor

---

*Genesis 47:27
†Genesis 16:12

for "the proud nomadic independence of the Ishmaelites," said one commentary.[2] Just as the patriarch Jacob used animal metaphors on his deathbed, declaring that one of his sons (Judah) would be a "lion's cub,"* another son (Issachar) a "rawboned donkey,"† another (Dan) a "serpent,"‡ still another (Naphtali) "a doe set free,"§ and his youngest (Benjamin) "a ravenous wolf,"¶ so it was entirely respectful for the angel to compare Ishmael to the rugged donkeys that roam the desert.

The nearest counterpart in American folklore would be the mustang—those wild ponies that run free across Nevada or Montana, finding their own food and surrendering to no man's control. That is Ishmael!

All of this was actually announced to a woman, Hagar, who literally *saw God.* At least that is what Hagar claimed: "I have now seen the One who sees me."** How many others could make such a statement?

It may also be observed that Ishmael was probably the first human being in history to receive the sign of God's covenant through circumcision. When God introduced this concept to Ishmael's father in Genesis 17 (along with the promise of another son yet to be born), the Scriptures tell us, "On that very day Abraham took his son Ishmael and all those born in his household or bought with his money, every male in his household, and circumcised them, as God told him. Abraham was ninety-nine years old when he was circumcised, and his son Ishmael was thirteen; Abraham and his son Ishmael were both circumcised on that same day."††

Given the discomfort of the procedure, it is likely that Abraham waited to go last! The young Ishmael was probably the first in line, bearing the physical mark of belonging to God. To this day, Arab

*Genesis 49:9
†Genesis 49:14
‡Genesis 49:17
§Genesis 49:21
¶Genesis 49:27
**Genesis 16:13
††Genesis 17:23-26

boys are circumcised—sometimes even as late as age thirteen, as Ishmael was. The Arabic word for it is *khitan.*

All of these things teach us that the Ishmaelite line is not a throwaway population in God's eyes. It was started under God's watchful care, received dramatic promises from him, began to multiply a full generation before that of Isaac (who had only two sons), and has today become a major beneficiary of God's resources (oil, natural gas, gems, spices). The hopes and dreams of this group are very real.

Granted, those hopes and dreams have not been well managed by a number of current Arab governments. Our politicians have betrayed us in numerous ways. We've been lied to time and again. The would-be peacemakers from the West have been purposely deceived and strung along. They have been told one thing by Arab leaders, only to see another unfold.

I believe this hurts the heart of God as deeply as it hurts the ordinary citizen. He never intended for us to be at swords' points with his people Israel. The sooner we realize that God has a plan for our *common good,* a way of living that will benefit us both, the sooner we all will realize his full blessing.

2. We must understand that the real bone of contention is not land; it is rejection.

The foremost Middle East question in most people's minds today is how to carve up the real estate. Where should the Jews live, and where should the Palestinians live? Should there be a "right of return" for those (or their descendants) who lost land in the 1948 shift, or not? Should Jewish settlements be allowed to exist in the West Bank, or not? How should the map be drawn?

Deeper than this, however, is a problem that one hundred million acres will not solve. It is not a new problem. It is as old as Abraham and his son.

When Abraham sent Hagar and Ishmael out of his household, he was by then a very rich man—yet he put them on the road with only "some food and a skin of water." How much? Only what he could "set . . . on her shoulders."* He didn't even provide a donkey or a tent! They began wandering in the desert and were soon on the verge of dehydration.

What a cheapskate Abraham was! Maybe he was afraid of what Sarah would say if he loaded them up with a caravan of supplies. At any rate, Ishmael—who as the firstborn son deserved to inherit a *double portion* of his father's estate, twice as much as Isaac would receive—was pushed off the ranch with virtually nothing.

There is a deeply significant word for what happened that day. It is *rejection*.

The problem that keeps Jews and Arabs on edge to this very time nearly four thousand years later is the same. It is the attitude that says, *You don't belong. I don't want you around. Just get out of here, will you? I don't take you seriously. If you starve to death or die of thirst, I don't really care. Get lost.*

Even Christians are in the habit of speaking about "the God of Abraham, Isaac, and Jacob"—which I fully recognize is a frequent phrase in the Old Testament. Certainly there's nothing wrong with that description per se. But the minute it is uttered, it inadvertently takes one side in this ancient family feud (the Isaac side) and ignores the other. Though the blessing for Abraham's son Isaac was obviously different, his son Ishmael also received a blessing. Leaving out this fact would be like leaving out all peoples but the English from the story of America's settlement. We must remember that our God is the God of Abraham, *Ishmael*, and Isaac. He had a plan for all the peoples who came from Abraham.

> There is a deeply significant word for what happened that day: *rejection*.

The terrorism and violence in today's world is the Arab way of screaming, "What about us? Don't we count for anybody's attention or respect?" I am not justifying these actions in the least. There are far better ways to resolve problems. But when you think about it,

*Genesis 21:14

after forty centuries this population is still trying to get recognition. Ishmael got pushed out of the camp of his father, Abraham—and his descendants today are still trying to get back in.

Fortunately for Ishmael and his mother, God did not dismiss them. The angel of God came to Hagar a second time. A well of water suddenly appeared out of nowhere. The mother and teenage son were rescued in the nick of time.

That wasn't the last provision of God for this now-single mom and her offspring. He continued to oversee their lives as the days and weeks became months and years. The biblical account concludes, "God was with the boy as he grew up. He lived in the desert and became an archer. While he was living in the Desert of Paran, his mother got a wife for him from Egypt,"* her original home.

God is in the business of *accepting* and *embracing* the people he lovingly created, not *rejecting* them. As long as we major in rejection, we will continue reaping a harvest of animosity, frustration, and death. Rejection is a dead-end street. We must approach this family feud in the Middle East with the open and generous heart of God in order to see it resolved.

How do we do that?

3. We need to stop pigeonholing Yasooa (Yeshua, *Jesus*) as merely the "Christian" voice in the debate. He is the Living Word for all *sides*.

As I've already mentioned, it was a shock for me at age forty-two to realize that Jesus (*Yasooa* in Arabic) was not a blond-haired, blue-eyed American. He was Jewish. He grew up going to synagogue. He no doubt had a bar mitzvah. He could hold his own debating the priests in the Jerusalem Temple.

When Charlie Sharpe told me Jesus was Jewish, it blew all my assumptions. I had never thought of him in that light. I wasn't sure I wanted to. But I couldn't deny the facts.

I had learned as a Muslim that Jesus was a prophet to be revered.

---

*Genesis 21:20-21

He wasn't mentioned very often by the imams, but whenever his name did come up, they spoke respectfully about him, as the Qur'an taught.

In the Middle Eastern discussion of our time, we need to stop sidelining Jesus as simply the founder of something called Christianity. He is God's unique Word to all in the midst of an emotional and noisy argument. He is clarity amid the posturing and distortion. He is the way, the truth, and the life.

He is a fresh perspective, just as he was when he first came to Palestine twenty centuries ago. "No one ever spoke the way this man does,"* said a squad of Temple guards sent to arrest him. They came back empty-handed. "The people were amazed at his teaching," wrote one biographer, "because he taught them as one who had authority, not as the teachers of the law."† He didn't fit into any neat little boxes.

> It was a shock for me at age forty-two to realize that Jesus was not a blond-haired, blue-eyed American.

In our present conflict, he dares to speak of reconciliation and even forgiveness. Before you write that off as wildly idealistic, look at what he accomplished in the ethnic tensions of the first century. Jews were at odds with their neighbors then just as fiercely as now. The issues were equally insoluble. Gentiles were despised—and all the more because they were the oppressors. Judea, Samaria, and Galilee were under the heavy hand of pagan Rome. The Jewish soul writhed in disgust over this. The derogatory phrase "Gentiles and tax-collectors" was common in their speech.‡ Tacitus, the Roman senator and historian, reported that Jews "regard the rest of mankind with all the hatred of enemies."§

Yet Jesus had come intending to be the Savior of the whole world. How would this ever come to pass?

---

*John 7:46
†Mark 1:22
‡See Matthew 18:17 *(New Revised Standard Version)* for one example.
§*Histories* vol. 5

The apostle Paul—a fervent Jew if there ever was one—explained it to a Gentile readership in the city of Ephesus:

> He himself is our peace, who has made the two one and has destroyed the barrier, the dividing wall of hostility, by abolishing in his flesh the law with its commandments and regulations. His purpose was to create in himself one new man out of the two, thus making peace, and in this one body to reconcile both of them to God through the cross, by which he put to death their hostility. He came and preached peace to you who were far away [*i.e., Gentiles*] and peace to those who were near [*i.e., Jews*]. For through him we both have access to the Father by one Spirit.
>   Consequently, you are no longer foreigners and aliens, but fellow citizens with God's people and members of God's household, built on the foundation of the apostles and prophets, with Christ Jesus himself as the chief cornerstone.*

If Jesus could accomplish this in the roiling, resentful climate of the first century, he can do it in the twenty-first. He can cleanse Palestinian hearts, Jewish hearts, Jordanian hearts, Saudi hearts, Egyptian hearts, Iraqi hearts, and all the rest of their prejudice and hatred. He can return us to the way he formed humanity in the first place, a divine creation in his hands that received the breath of life from his loving attention.

Jesus is not so interested in building a *religion* as he is in building *relationships* that honor his plan for the world. These relationships are both vertical, with him, and horizontal, with our fellow human beings. When my heart is clean and I have a relationship with Jesus, it is easier to have a peaceful relationship with my neighbor.

Granted, the societies of the Middle East may never be a "melting pot" in the sense of the American ideal. (Many would say that America isn't really a melting pot either, but more like a tossed salad, with each component retaining its identity.) Israelis want a

---

*Ephesians 2:14-20

Jewish society. I understand that and accept their wishes. Palestinians want a Muslim society. In fact, they expect Jesus to return someday as a Muslim and lead the world to Islam!

Regardless of this diversity, Jesus is our one hope of reconciliation in the here and now. He is the only one I can think of who holds the power, the moral authority, to bring us together. He is the antidote to mistrust and bitterness and resentment. He is the one who convinces an Arab like me that the Jews are not my enemies but rather my cousins, going back to Abraham's house. That puts a whole different light on the subject. No wonder the ancient prophet, seven hundred years ahead of time, called him the "Prince of Peace."*

> Jesus is our one hope of reconciliation in the here and now.

4. Finally, we need to begin feeling each other's pain.

When we watch the news and see the anguish of yet another untimely funeral in Jerusalem or in Gaza, in Tel Aviv or in Nablus, we need to recall the words of the compassionate Jesus:

> Blessed are those who mourn, for they will be comforted.
> Blessed are the merciful, for they will be shown mercy.
> Blessed are the peacemakers, for they will be called sons
>   of God.†

We need to see the Jewish Jesus stopping to care for a Gentile centurion with a critically ill servant. He listens to the prognosis and promptly replies, "I will go and heal him."‡

The reality of human pain cuts across all categories, ideologies, and political parties. It forces us together in a community of suffering. It transcends who is "right" and who is "wrong." It demands that we become human and responsive once again.

---

*Isaiah 9:6
†Matthew 5:4, 7, 9
‡Matthew 8:7

In 2007, my wife and I met a Jewish woman named Sarai* who lives in Jerusalem and has known the sting of Middle Eastern violence. Her son, Lior, was called to the Israeli army at age eighteen. Two years later, he caught a ride one day with a civilian worker who was leaving the base where he was stationed. No more than two hundred meters outside the gate, they were attacked by a mob of Palestinian students looking for an Israeli soldier to lynch.

A rock smashed the driver's side window of the small car. The driver jumped out and ran back toward the base to get help. Lior, meanwhile, was temporarily knocked unconscious. By the time he came around again, he had been pulled out of the car by the mob and subjected to a horrible beating. He felt his weapon being torn away from him. Both knees were broken, several ribs cracked, his head was badly lacerated, and he sustained damage to his eyes that would prove to be permanent.

Somehow he managed to get away and was soon recovered by army reinforcements. However, his ordeal was not yet finished. The army, in public statements to the media, criticized Lior for not resisting the attackers and at least wounding some of them. He was portrayed as a wimp. The young man came home humiliated.

Sarai watched her son retreat into his bedroom for a full year, rarely coming out. His mental torment lasted long after his physical wounds had healed. Any news of a bus bombing or other incident would send him further into withdrawal, sleeping for twenty-four hours straight. The happy, well-adjusted son she had raised was gone.

"I became furious at what had befallen him," Sarai told us. "It was so unfair. He had gone to serve his country and been victimized twice—first by the mob, second by the army." She described one particularly poignant quarrel with God.

"Sarai, is it so hard for you to forgive?"

"Yes, it is! It's impossible."

Again came the words: "Is it so hard for you to forgive?"

---

* The names in this story have been changed to protect the family's identity.

Exasperated, she replied, "Lord, what do you want? Do you know how hard that is?"

"Yes, I know. I watched my own Son be beaten and even killed by a vicious crowd."

At that, this mother broke down. "Abba," she prayed, "please give me your ability to release this terrible weight. I can't do it by myself. Give me your compassion." A torrent of anger and resentment drained out of her that day. It was a freeing moment for her.

Today, Sarai organizes summer camps for children who have lost family members to suicide bombings. She teaches that hatred is sin—something that is simply not acceptable to a holy God. It must be released, or it will eat us away.

She also moderates a group for widows of those killed by the violence. She told them about me—and in response, they asked to meet me. I walked into the room that evening apprehensive about what would take place. Sarai introduced me and asked me to tell my story.

I shared the facts as carefully as I could, not wanting to open fresh wounds in their hearts after what they had already lived through. I told how the Lord had turned my life in a new direction through his grace.

When I finished, the floor was opened for questions. These women, whose husbands had been murdered by the likes of me in earlier days, did not hold back. They grilled me with such inquiries as

"Did you send terrorists here to Israel?"

"Do you have blood on your hands?"

"Have you personally killed Jews?"

I had to tell the truth. I admitted what I had done as a Fatah fighter. I added, "The Lord has forgiven me, but I still live with my conscience. I cannot get away from the scenes of death that I caused."

Sensing the pain in their minds, I asked them for their forgiveness. In response, they talked about how hatred and rage had run wild in their emotions after their husbands' violent deaths. But then they had come to recognize the true source of blame. It was not so much individuals as it was the Islamist brainwashing to which we had been subjected. Their demeanor began to thaw as they expressed their pardon toward me.

At the end of the meeting, they asked Sarai, "Can we hug him?"

"Yes, you certainly may," she replied.

They gathered around, begging me to stay safe and work in places not so dangerous as the Gaza Strip. I told them, "I must go where God is sending me. But let me ask you to please pray for me and pray for this work of reconciliation." They promised they would do so.

Miraculous scenes like this one are possible when we let down our guard enough to feel what the other person is feeling. Often our opponents carry their own burdens of pain. When we take that pain seriously, the road to reconciliation starts to open up.

TOGETHER AGAIN

The children of Ishmael and the children of Isaac have lived close to each other in this region from ancient times. This is how it has been, and it is how it should remain. Through the peace that comes from Yasooa/Yeshua/Jesus, we can recover the family relationship that has been lost. We can build bridges to one another. We can accept each other—despite our differences—instead of loading heaps of rejection upon each other.

The Bible tells how our two forefathers laid aside their bad memories and came together at the death of Abraham. "Altogether, Abraham lived a hundred and seventy-five years. Then Abraham breathed his last and died at a good old age, an old man and full of years; and he was gathered to his people. His sons Isaac and Ishmael buried him in the cave of Machpelah near Mamre."*

I love that mental picture of Ishmael, now eighty-nine years old, and his half-brother Isaac, now seventy-five, working side by side to conduct a proper burial for their father. The years have softened them both, no doubt. Gray has come into their hair. Both their mothers—the two women who clashed so spectacularly—are gone by now, we assume; Sarah has been dead for almost four decades,

*Genesis 25:7-9

and Hagar is nowhere to be seen in the current story. It's just the two sons, doing the right thing for their father, not letting history detract from the moment when family members ought to be together.

Is it too much to expect the same here in our time? I do not think so. We can make life in the Middle East work again through the intervention of the One who said, "With man this is impossible, but with God all things are possible."*

---

*Matthew 19:26

CHAPTER 19

FOR
US
ALL

OTHER PEOPLE'S ARGUMENTS SEEM EASIER TO SOLVE. We look down from our personal mountaintop of wisdom and say, "If only they would be reasonable about this," or "Well, they need to meet each other halfway." With dispassionate objectivity we analyze the various factors and declare a logical compromise that "anybody" should be able to accept.

But when it comes to our own disagreements and complaints, things are not so simple. We get aggravated with those closest to us: our spouses, our children, our parents, our in-laws. *They're being so self-centered*, we tell ourselves. *They don't care about me or my point of view.* Here in the center of our daily lives, often under our own roofs, we are frustrated with relationships that were meant to bring joy and fulfillment.

The family represents the hub in a set of concentric circles. Our next circle moving outward from the center contains the associations to which we formally belong: our workplaces, our churches, perhaps our schools. We spend a number of hours every week in these places. Here again, we run into people who irritate us. The boss who makes irrational demands . . . the pastor or lay leader who doesn't listen to our input . . . the teacher or principal who seems agenda driven. We'd like to straighten them out—but how? They're too stubborn to yield, we say.

The third circle represents all those people we encounter more incidentally who are simply different from us. They may be of a different ethnic group. They may be of a different generation. They may be female while we are male, or vice versa. Their political loyalties are unlike ours. Their education may be inferior to ours—or, on the other hand, it may be vastly above ours, which intimidates us. At any rate, they don't think as we do. They don't value the things we believe are truly important. They get under our skin.

All of these sore spots are hard to recognize because we are so close to them. It's far easier to look at a conflict seven or eight thousand miles away—Jews versus Palestinians, for example, or Shiites versus Sunnis—and see what *they* should be doing or should stop doing. But when the trouble festers in the inner circles of our own lives, we have to work harder at pursuing peace.

I find it curious that a church can invite me to come speak about reconciliation in the Middle East—when it is not reconciled with the church just down the block. The subject of reconciliation is in vogue these days, as long as it deals with *somebody else*. It is harder for all of us to face our own needs to clear away the barriers.

Muslims are genuinely perplexed by the disunity they see across the Christian landscape. They cannot understand why the followers of Jesus find so much to disagree about. They see it as a weakness of our faith that they can exploit. And their questioning should not be brushed aside.

RECONCILIATION TAKES TIME

One of the things I have learned over the past fifteen years is that reconciliation and harmony take time to grow. Not often do we see an instant fix, the way I suddenly lost my hatred for Jews within a day of my conversion. That was indeed a miracle, for which I thank God. But it was an exception to the way things normally evolve.

People say of their adversaries, "I don't mind so-and-so. I just don't trust them." Trust is a fragile bloom that develops slowly, gradually. With nurturing, it can grow from a tiny shoot into a large and sturdy plant. In the early stages, however, its potential can be stunted by a chill wind or careless footstep.

My daughter, Farah, took a long time to accept me as her father once I returned from my eighteen-month "exile" in California. She was twelve years old when I left, a teenager when I returned. I had missed a lot of basketball games and school concerts in the meantime. Farah had learned to count on her mother and assume I was unreliable.

> Not often do we see an instant fix, the way I suddenly lost my hatred for Jews within a day of my conversion.

When she would ask Karen for permission to do something and Karen would defer to me for a decision, it would irritate her. What gave me the right to be in charge of anything? She saw me as unworthy, a dropout dad.

She was fifteen and a half when I gave my life to Christ. That did nothing to relieve the anger toward me that smoldered inside her. In fact, it tampered with her identity as a Muslim girl, as I mentioned previously. Farah's passions run deep, and when something stirs her anger, it can last a long time.

I couldn't talk her out of her opinion about me. I could only live a responsible life before her, trying to the best of my ability to follow and demonstrate what I read in my Bible. I sought to be reliable and show integrity in all I did. The only other thing I could do was pray for a healing of this relationship.

In time my daughter came to realize that she could trust Christ. But her dad was still suspect in her eyes. I remember the weekend Karen was away with a friend, leaving just the two of us alone in the house. Farah didn't want to have to interact with me. She thought up a string of places to go and friends to visit—anything to be apart from me. I saw her only when she stopped by to change clothes. Then she was out the door again.

She was into her early twenties before she finally let go of the resentment I had triggered. Our relationship today is marvelously restored. In fact, she works with Karen and me in the Hope for Ishmael office, along with her other responsibilities as a youth dormitory manager at Heartland.

"My former dad—that person doesn't exist anymore," she now says. "He and I listen to each other. We talk about everything. I learn new things about him every time I hear him speak to an audience. Our relationship has become a wonderful thing in both our lives.

"The truth is, Dad and I are very much alike. We're both very Arab. When people tell me I'm like my dad, I beam with pride. I love and respect him with all my heart."

But this reconciliation did not come quickly. It required the combination of faithful living on my part and God's touch deep inside of her. The process took a full five years.

Ben, my son, came around faster, probably because he was already a believer in Christ—and afraid of my reaction—when I surprised him with my own news that first morning. This tended to override the neglect he had experienced from me. Now married and the father of three little girls, Ben is the kind of attentive dad I was not. It is a joy to see. I'm so proud of him.

A couple of years ago on his blog, Ben posted a Father's Day tribute that brought tears to my eyes. He talked about how much he appreciated my adopting him. He called me a "hero for the complete surrender to God that he has. . . . He's dodged bullets, been spit upon by Muslim clerics, chastised by his culture—all to serve the living God. My dad is a true 'Indiana Jones.'" (That's one of our family's favorite movie characters.) "Happy Father's Day, Dad!"

This kind of outcome could happen only by the grace of God working in all our lives over a period of time. I will be forever humbled and grateful that the bad seeds I sowed in earlier times were neutralized. As the Lord said through the prophet Joel, "I will repay you for the years the locusts have eaten . . . and you will praise the name of the LORD your God, who has worked wonders for you."* That has certainly proved true in our case, and I thank the Lord for his goodness.

DROP THE LIST

What Farah and Ben have experienced is that we all need to break the resentments that can build up in our lives. We have to let go of our assumptions and conclusions. We have to let go of our lists of grievances. We have to recognize that we, too, have agendas that aggravate the situation.

The apostle James got to the heart of the matter when he wrote, "What causes fights and quarrels among you? Don't they come from your desires that battle within you? You want something but don't get it. You kill and covet, but you cannot have what you want. You quarrel and fight. You do not have, because you do not ask God. When you ask, you do not receive, because you ask with wrong motives, that you may spend what you get on your pleasures."†

Ken Sande, president of Peacemaker Ministries, unfolds this passage with these words:

> Conflicts arise from unmet desires in our hearts. When we feel we cannot be satisfied unless we have something we want or think we need, the desire turns into a demand. If someone fails to meet that desire, we condemn him in our heart and quarrel and fight to get our way. In short, conflict arises when *desires* grow into *demands* and we *judge* and *punish* those who get in our way.[1]

Our fervent desire, Sande says with frankness, can actually be an idol. "Most of us think of an idol as a statue of wood, stone, or metal worshiped by pagan people. But the concept is much broader and far more personal than that. An idol is anything apart from God that we depend on to be happy, fulfilled, or secure."[2]

When we think we *must* have a certain outcome to be happy,

---

*Joel 2:25-26
†James 4:1-3

fulfilled, or secure, we are prone to clash with anything or anyone who gets in our way. God, meanwhile, is in the business of smashing idols. He is the only One worthy of our worship. When we focus on him, when we truly believe he is the sum total of all we actually need, the cause of conflict goes away.

When I speak to groups of messianic Jews, I often say, "A soul is worth more than land. To bring a single Palestinian soul to Jesus is more important than hanging onto acreage." When I address Arab Christians, I make the same point in reverse. "So far, most Jews are not finding their true Messiah. For us to bring them in that direction is worth far more in God's eyes than proving our point about the land."

Whatever the conflict on whatever continent, we must never lose sight of what God considers important. He is "not wanting anyone to perish"—whether Palestinian, Jew, your irritating neighbor, your son, your daughter, or your worst enemy—"but everyone to come to repentance."* He is more concerned about this than about our being right or getting what we consider to be justice.

When we think we *must* have a certain outcome to be happy, fulfilled, or secure, we are prone to clash with anything or anyone who gets in our way.

There is no magic formula for bringing about reconciliation. In the complex realm of human feelings, disputes are often too entrenched for mechanical fixes. We need God's healing touch to smooth the sandpaper in our personalities. When I first came to the Lord, I read the whole Bible in forty-five days—and the verses that stuck in my mind more than any others were Proverbs 3:5-6. "Trust in the LORD with all your heart and lean not on your own understanding; in all your ways acknowledge him, and he will make your paths straight."

This is the key to right living—"Trust in the LORD." Every time I find myself in a sticky situation, I seem to hear the Lord saying,

*2 Peter 3:9

"Trust me." For every conflict in which we become embroiled, the answer lies not so much in our own understanding as in relying, trusting, leaning upon the Lord. That is how the crooked paths become straight—in our families, our communities, and across our world.

LIGHTING UP THE BLIND SPOTS

When God is allowed to plant his peace in our hearts, we can then influence others in the same direction. We become peacemakers. We get the chance to illuminate blind spots that are blocking reconciliation.

I was riding in a taxi one time in Gaza where several other passengers were present. I looked out at the traffic and commented to the driver, "So many taxis! You have a lot of competition, don't you?"

"Yes, it's really out of control," he said. "Everybody who owns a car wants to get into the business now. Soon there are going to be more drivers than passengers." He sighed.

> When God is allowed to plant his peace in our hearts, we can then influence others in the same direction. We become peacemakers.

Then he continued, "When the Israelis were in control, it wasn't like this. Everything was more organized then."

Right away a man jumped into the discussion from the backseat. "Well, no! No—just think about it. The Jews want to kill every Muslim in the world! Even their holy books tell them to do it!" he insisted.

I could have just let the comment pass. But I didn't. I looked over my shoulder and said, "Really? Have you read their books? Did they really say that?"

"Yes, absolutely!" the man replied. "I haven't read them myself, but that's what our imams say."

"Well, I've read the holy books of the Jews," I answered, "and I don't remember anything there about killing Muslims."

"The imams have to be right," the man retorted. "They know they will answer to Allah for what they say."

"But does it make sense?" I asked. "How could that command be in the Torah? Back when it was written by the prophet Moses, there was no Islam at all. Islam came along after Moses and David and the Lord Jesus Christ. So how could the ancient books say that Muslims should be murdered?"

The passenger was taken aback. "What? Judaism existed *before* Islam?"

"Yes, my friend," I said. "Read it for yourself. Don't believe everything a man with a long beard tells you. When you study Jewish history, you find that they win Nobel prizes for medical inventions that sustain life. On the other hand, what do we produce these days? Suicide bombers!"

"You sound like a clever man. Where do you get your knowledge?"

"From the Bible."

"Oh! So you're a Christian?"

"Yes, I am."

"I've never seen a Christian before."

Now it was my turn to be surprised. "You've really never met a Christian in all of Gaza?" I asked.

"No. I didn't even know there were Christians in this city."

"Well, there are not many," I admitted. "But we are here. We want to help make this a better place for everyone."

The man thought for a minute. "Where can I get a copy of your holy book?" he then asked. "I would like to read it for myself."

I assured him I could help him with that request.

The One who came to this world to bring peace and reconciliation is as active today as he was two thousand years ago. He is speaking to open hearts and minds through the Scripture, for those who can acquire a copy or read it on the Internet. He is appearing especially to Muslims through dreams and visions. He is offering his gift of forgiveness across all lands and cultures. He is welcoming every human being who will ask to enter his family. And once inside, we have the high privilege of extending the Good News to those who are wondering what Jesus is all about.

It took me forty-two years to "make the connection." My hope and prayer is that others will not have to wait that long. The forces of hatred and animosity can be dismantled through the loving touch of the One who came "to reconcile to himself all things, whether things on earth or things in heaven, by making peace through his blood, shed on the cross. Once you were alienated from God and were enemies in your minds because of your evil behavior. But now he has reconciled you. . . . This is the gospel that you heard and that has been proclaimed to every creature under heaven."*

Good news, indeed.

---

*Colossians 1:20-23

NOTES

Chapter 2: The Making of a Troublemaker

1. Ruby, Robert, "A Six-Day War: Its Aftermath in American Public Opinion," Pew Forum on Religion & Public Life, May 30, 2007, http://pewforum.org/docs/?DocID=218. Curiously, European and Asian nations are sharply different from the United States on this question. Examples include, with Israeli sympathies appearing first, Palestinian second Great Britain 24–29; France 38–38; Spain 9–32; India 20–22.

Chapter 5: Young Warrior

1. Gideon Rafael, *Destination Peace: Three Decades of Israeli Foreign Policy: A Personal Memoir* (London: Weidenfield and Nicolson, 1981), 203.

Chapter 18: For the Middle East

1. *Zondervan TNIV Study Bible* (Grand Rapids, MI: Zondervan, 2006), 32.
2. *The New Bible Commentary: Revised* (Grand Rapids, MI: Eerdmans, 1970), 96.

Chapter 19: For Us All

1. Sande, Ken, "Getting to the Heart of Conflict," posted on www.peacemaker.net; adapted from his book *Peacemaking for Families* (Wheaton, IL: Tyndale, 2002), italics added.
2. Ibid.

ABOUT THE AUTHORS

TASS SAADA is a former Muslim and founder of Hope for Ishmael, a nonprofit organization whose mission is to reconcile Arabs and Jews. Born in 1951 in the Gaza Strip, Saada grew up in Saudi Arabia and Qatar. He worked under Yasser Arafat as a Fatah fighter and sniper. Years after immigrating to America, he became a Christian.

DEAN MERRILL has been published in over forty magazines and has coauthored more than twenty-six books. Some of his well-known titles are *To Fly Again* and *New York Times* best seller *In the Presence of My Enemies,* both written with Philippine missionary and terrorist-abduction survivor Gracia Burnham.

Since this book was first released, my wife and I have founded a new organization called Seeds of Hope, a registered 501(c)(3), which works to make a difference in the lives of children and families throughout the Middle East. This represents the bulk of our current work, and our desire is to bring long-term change to families through education, economic development, cultural exchange, and humanitarian aid.

If you have been inspired by my life, please consider supporting Seeds of Hope. Visit our website at www.seedsofhope.org to learn more about what we are doing to serve the people of the Middle East and to help heal the land.

Many thanks,
Taysir Abu Saada